A
Moment
With

A Moment With *Bev*

A Loving Guide for Coping, Caring & Sharing

BEVERLY WADE AACH

PENTLAND PRESS, INC.
ENGLAND · USA · SCOTLAND

PUBLISHED BY PENTLAND PRESS, INC.
5124 Bur Oak Circle, Raleigh, North Carolina 27612
United States of America
919-782-0281

ISBN 1-57197-071-1
Library of Congress Catalog Card Number 97-67140

Printed in the United States of America

To my husband, and to all of those who encouraged me to sit down and put my thoughts into words.

Table of Contents

Foreword

It is amazing how a book just happens! With the encouragement of family and friends, I have written some of my thoughts and prayers that I want to share with you. Life guarantees a few knocks as you go along the way and I seem to have had my share of those. However, there have been many, many blessings, too. I have had to develop some methods of coping. There have been a few flashes of inspiration, some thoughts and prayers and bits of philosophy. These I should like to share with you. I have added a story or two, a few of the true miracles in my life and some memories that are very special to me! I truly pray that you will find that Special Prayer for that Special Occasion or those special words to say to someone who needs them . . . I have found my joy in the writing of them . . .

Lovingly,

Bevie

Daydreaming With Bev

It is a beautiful spring morning in St. Louis, and I am taking my cup of hot chocolate outdoors to sit in the warm sunshine. I dream, relax, renew my love of life and thank God for giving me this day as I sit here and let my thoughts go hither and thither with no thought of order or tidiness. I would like to share some of these random thoughts with you.

Why did I have such terrible dreams last night?

Fear takes hold of us in the night and in strange places when we are alone, but God says, "Fear not, for I am with you."(Isiah 43:05) He also says, "And lo! I will be with you always, to the end of the age."(Matthew 28:16) What man is fool enough to choose problems and troubles over trust in the Lord? We must put our faith in Him and live our days one at a time, knowing that He is with us, and He loves us. Christ's message in all its richness must live in our hearts. Can you remember who first told you about God, or have you always known Him?

I love the old Cherokee Indian blessing: "May the warm winds of heaven blow softly on your house and may the Great Spirit bless all who enter there." I feel so strongly about the warmth and love in a home that we had our home blessed as soon as possible after we had moved in! I can feel the love in it, and I hope that if you come to visit, you will also feel the love and warmth here.

I pray in the morning—do you? I hope that I have been a blessing in someone else's life by perhaps shining a ray of light in the darkness or saying word of encouragement at just the right time. It may have been only a smile of friendship, but I hope it was there and appreciated!

A winner feels responsible for more than his job. A loser says, "I only work here." This phrase really says everything, doesn't it? I wish that everyone who works for a living could read it, too!

A note of humor to lighten your day: A little boy came home dejected from his first day of school. "Ain't goin' tomorrow," he said. "Why not, dear?" his mother asked. The little boy replied, "Well, I can't read 'n I can't write 'n they won't let me talk—so what's the use?"

Today, as I understand it, children can talk as much as they want! I can't quite figure out when they listen! Or even if they ever do listen!

Here are some rules for happiness: Have something to do, someone to love, and something to hope for. This also says it all, doesn't it? Every active person has all of this. Our thoughts and prayers must go to those who do not!

I ask the Lord to help me to practice the art of sunny living, make me always give a warm handclasp and speak cheerfully. Aid me in finding the beautiful amid the ugly and grant me the divine sunshine of Thy kingdom and send me forth each day to share its glow. Make me wise to know that "a merry heart does good like medicine." Help me to have faith, practice patience, radiate cheer and live love. Keep me strong in spirit and confident of heart.

This is my prayer for you today. So when the sun sets taking the lights and its beautiful colors, may we have so lived the day that we can say, "Dear Lord, I thank Thee for this day! Help me to live each day well, knowing that each day has so many, many blessings that I cannot begin to count them."

God Bless!

A Giver or A Taker?

I must ask myself this question: "Do I give because I want to, because I feel that I have to, or because people expect me to?" This is a difficult question for me to answer because I have always considered myself to be a giver. I love to give people things. By things, I mean gifts, food, clothing, and things that I own and love. That does sound nice, doesn't it?

But then, I have to ask myself, "Why do I get such pleasure from the giving? Is it because I want people to like me?" The answer to that is yes, but I really don't think that is the main reason. I think that when someone else is happy, then I, too, am happy. Yes, really! A stranger's smile does wonderful things for me. I go my way smiling and feeling good, and I would guess that is because I feel that they feel good, too.

In some ways, I shy away from the negative side of reality that I know is there. But when I have to face it, I can and do. I have found, although, that if I put things off for a while, they never go away. They always stay in the back of my mind. When push comes to shove, I am ready to deal with the problems, the loss, or whatever mountain there is to climb. In the meantime, I keep on giving. In the final reality, sometimes I keep getting hurt because either they don't want what I have to give, or they take it for granted that I will continue to give.

Does that mean that I am also a taker? I must answer that frankly and say that, although I don't know for sure, I really do not think so! It embarrasses me to receive too much (I don't often have this problem), and I'm never really sure whether they are giving because they want to, or because they feel that they owe me!

I just reread that sentence and it reads as if I have a real hang-up, does it not? I have many friends that I love to be with even though I have learned through hurt feelings that they never really give of themselves. I can find many excuses for them, for I really love them, but I have to wonder if they have been conditioned from childhood to take and expect. I really think that they have. I have also learned that some people expect these "gifts," because they feel that they deserve everything and usually get it!

When I have to question someone's giving or taking, it makes me very unhappy. I do really love a "fairy-tale world" and don't like to face the fact that there are some folks out there who are not very nice at all. There are some who are just cold emotionally or, at least, that is the impression that they give to the world and to the people they meet. I have often wondered how these people act toward their loved ones. It is strange, isn't it, how different people are!

Think about yourself while you are driving somewhere or waiting in the doctor's office or the office of the dentist. Are you a giver or a taker? The perfect way to be would be a little of both or the middle of the road. At any rate, it should be an interesting thing to think about and mull over in your mind. I can't say whether either is good or bad. Everyone must do as he or she wants. More to the point, they must do whatever his or her conscience or belief dictates and whatever makes them comfortable, happy and able to live in serenity.

Whatever conclusion or decision, God loves you. You are a very special person, an individual who can believe, vote, give or take. You can be free and happy, as long as you observe the rights and the wrongs, be your own person, proud of yourself, considerate of your fellow man, and true to your beliefs. Be grateful for that and for the fact that you are in this country where ideals, beliefs and goals are admired and supported! God bless this country of ours and make us grateful that we live here!

God Bless!

Judging Others

I returned home from a small card party today very confused about what I really felt about judging other people with whom I come in contact. Usually, I have a firm belief about right or wrong, but today I had to take a backward step and think about the incident and judgments in general.

I attend a weekly bridge group. I love every one of these young girls, young matrons and women in my age bracket! We have a beautiful rapport! We share parts of our lives with each other! We cry on shoulders, ask for prayers in times of trouble or illness, give advice, sympathize or do whatever is needed. In other words, we support each other with love and understanding.

One particular day, one of our group had had a bad start to the day. We all felt very badly about it, but some of us (me for one) had some problems of our own to solve— "bridges to cross"—before being free to attend the bridge party. Our friend just could not forget the terrible beginning to her day and was almost ill. When we suggested that she lie down, she refused. The card party went on, but she could not relax. As a result, everyone felt depressed and sad! When your friends hurt, you hurt too!

That evening I told my husband about it and asked him if he thought I should just give up the bridge parties. My free time is limited, and I only go to relax with close friends and enjoy. He said "Bevie, don't let one happening spoil this wonderful rapport you have with these girls. Just forget about one day and go on." And so I did. I really like this friend very much. She is vibrant, a little excitable perhaps, but lovely!

Driving home today from bridge club, I started thinking about our quickness to judge others. We really do not know what stress they might be under, what pain they might be having or what has occurred that very day to upset them. I believe that we all have a tendency to judge others if we don't understand them or agree with them. Even when they deserve to be "set down" a little, it really isn't our place to sit in judgment, is it?

I feel that one of my worst faults is judging and correcting others. I do not know why or when I started doing this, but it is terribly wrong of me! I am often ashamed, sorry or just upset with myself but somehow not sorry enough to change this fault! I promise myself to try, but it is really difficult to do.

I always think of the song, "You Always Hurt the One You Love." This is so true. We don't criticize strangers (not to their faces) because we want everyone to love us or at least to like us. We know our family will love us even if we criticize them. But that's not really fair, is it?

When I look around and pay special attention, I see that all human beings tend to judge on hearsay, what they read in the paper, or simply judge by their own standards. I am not confusing my statement with right or wrong—this is completely different. To live happily in this world, you have to have rules to go by and punishment for wrongdoings such as violence, murder, theft, and so forth. This I agree with. Some people do not seem to be able to judge things for themselves and are easily led. Sometimes these same people serve on juries, and that, too, is bad. They should not be on any jury unless they can make their own decisions.

So, what can I say about judging others? Only God can be the true judge about your decisions. Time can tell you whether they were right or wrong. By that time it is too late, and you have to live with the decision you have made. I pray that I will be more tolerant in my attitude toward the decisions of others. Usually, I become overly critical because I care so much. I don't want to see those I love make the same mistakes I made (forgetting that nothing is ever quite the same).

So, I pray for those I love. They must be free to make their own decisions without being judged by those who love them. If you have a clear conscience, integrity, honesty, love and compassion you have it all, and it does not matter about the judgments of others!

Be true to yourself and remember, when you are upset with those judging you, just be sure you have not committed the same offense. I think that most of us have!

God Bless!

Coping With Problems

It has been said that a cheerful heart is a good medicine, but a downcast spirit dries up the bones. This really sounds good, but what do you do when everything has gone wrong? Sometimes there is a cloudy day and you feel ignored, rejected, unloved and depressed, just because of things in general. This is a very difficult subject to address. I believe that everyone has found his or her own way to deal with this problem by the time they reach maturity, and, if they have not, they probably never will.

I do not know whether professional advice can help or not, but I was told by my personal physician that some people just cannot cope! Children need advice and suggestions from their parents and loved ones to help them along life's way. Life is not at all easy, even for the most fortunate. I personally put "on hold" any problem that I cannot find the answer to. I do this by prayer, picking up a good book, calling a friend on the telephone (not to discuss problems) to hear a friendly, caring voice—anything to shelve the problem for the time being!

A little breathing space does wonders, and sometimes it lets you look at things in a different way. Sometimes the problem just goes away by itself, and, if it does not, I recite my many blessings to myself. First of all, I say, "Bev, you are not bedridden, you do not have an incurable disease, you are not in terrible pain, and you are coping. You have a loving family, a wonderful, caring husband, so many blessings that you cannot count them! Best of all, you have friends to share your blessings with."

Sometimes, it isn't easy when your problems magnify and pile up. You look around and see people who don't seem to have any problems at all and seem to never have had any. You must remember that God has a plan, and He is with us every minute of every day. All problems, large or small, are important to Him! Talk to Him, tell Him your troubles and ask for strength to cope with them. You cannot wish yourself to be in another person's place. You have to find the best way on your own. Abraham Lincoln said, "Most folks are about as happy as they make up their minds to be." Many people miss their share of happiness, not because they never found it, but because they didn't stop to enjoy it!

Do take time to help others. Remember, it is only by forgetting yourself that you draw nearer to God. Ask Him to show you the way! Ask Him how to grow in spirit, strength, and prayer! Remember, your friends do not like to be around you if you complain constantly, even though they love you. Try to be pleasant and cheerful. Keep a happy smile handy for someone who needs you. I firmly believe that we need lots of love and laughter in our lives. We also need to have compassion, sincere interest and a desire to be of service to our fellow man as well as to our loved ones. We must help our friends and loved ones count their many blessings (everyone has many) and forget their misfortunes (everyone has some of those, too). It is said that happiness is not created by what happens to us but by our attitude toward each happening. When things look their darkest and your problems seem too big to handle, say a prayer of courage. Then, throw back your shoulders, stand strong, hold your head high, take a deep breath, smile and take that first big step forward.

Congratulations! You are coping!

God Bless!

Hope

Our subject for thought today as we stretch our bodies and strive for flexibility of mind is hope. Can't cope? Try hope! My exercise class liked this message, and I hope you do, too!

A gesture of love many times ignites a spark of hope, and even a tiny whisper of hope can set us spinning in a positive direction. Doctors respect it as powerful medicine and surgeons are leery of operating on people who do not have it. Hope sustains us through petty crises and real adversity. I should like to make two special points while I am talking to you today.

1. Most people never give up hoping.
2. There is an art to hoping, and we can all learn it.

Hope is the expectation that tomorrow will be better than today. When hope transcends reality or persists against all odds, it turns into faith—faith in God, faith in oneself, faith in mankind. Hope can save a life, and it can relieve pain. Almost one hundred years ago, a philosopher wrote, "He who has a why to live for, can bear with almost any how."

Pessimism feeds on bad news while hope breeds optimism. Find your own silver lining; don't wallow in self pity. Learn to laugh! Hope is contagious, so borrow from others. Practice faith and practice daydreaming.

Are you an optimist?

1. Do you wake up curious about what the day will bring?
2. Do you picture yourself a winner?
3. Have you someone to whom you can tell your troubles?
4. Can you laugh at yourself? Try it! Life will be a joy with faith, hope and a genuine love of others.

Laugh and hope, and live every minute of every day!

God Bless!

Take Time

Sometimes, when I sit down to share my thoughts and prayers with you, I wonder what I should talk about. God seems to take over my thoughts and tell me what to say. We really have almost the same problems and worries, do we not? It is marvelous to speak always of joy and happiness. That is, after all, one large and important goal in our lives.

But to have this joy and peace within ourselves, we must cope with what life gives to us along the way and do it as well as we can, doing what we think God would want us to do. God has said to me, "Slow down Bevie." What does he say to you? Do you take the time to listen?

When I received my message, I wondered if perhaps I spent too much time working with my various philanthropic and patriotic organizations. I enjoy them, it is true, and they need me, but am I taking enough time to spend by myself, with my family and with God? These are the most important things in life: your family and God. Committee work is very vital, but is like a low, soft chair; easy to get into but so hard to get out of. We must take time to meditate, worship, pray and care for those who need our prayers and help so very badly.

Consider these suggestions.

Take time to be kind to your parents. They need your love, and perhaps they are lonely. They have spent most of their adult lives taking care of you, educating you, sending you to college if they could, and worrying about you and your future. After you are married and have moved away from home, they feel lost and not needed. This reminder is not meant to depress you at all but to remind you that we must take time to enjoy our families who care, friends who care and a House of God that is so welcoming that we are reassured once again that He cares!

Sometimes you get lonely for that special someone to share thoughts, worries and joys with. You can then realize that you are not alone, and God is always there. So take time to pray. Pray for the homeless and the hungry. Resolve to be a supplier to them from your own food shelves, not just on the holidays but on other days as well.

Take time to be a supplier of friendship and love. Remember that every life has its burdens and that no one has everything. Take time to listen, to be more understanding of your loved ones and to keep from asking more of them than they are able to give.

Take time to remind yourself that you are God's child and that he loves you just as you are. We need to do this especially when we have been unjustly accused or corrected. Take time to pray for help to restore your self esteem.

Take time to ask God to teach you not to want what someone else has. It is wrong to envy others for their worldly possessions and for the peace and happiness they have found in their lives. Do we have any idea of what they might have overcome with the help of God to reach this peace and joy that they have?

Take time to ask the Lord to help you in your difficult decisions. Everyone fears having to live with wrong choices, so you must ask Him to be your advisor and to help you. All of us have opportunities every day to show our appreciation and love to someone.

Take time to think of others, share your thoughts, your cares and your love. Take time every day to make a quick telephone call or send a card to a sick friend. These thoughts are called "sharing and caring."

Time is such a valuable thing, impossible to see or to feel, but using it wisely is such an important part of our lives that we cannot take it for granted. Don't let your time run out before you take time to share and care and enjoy what you are so blessed to have.

God Bless!

Legacy of Laughter & Love

I was sitting in the funeral parlor with my son-in-law and his family, and we were reminiscing about Don's mother. Estate details were discussed, but I tried not to listen to those for they weren't my business. Suddenly, Don's sister-in-law, Melba, turned to me and asked, "When you die, Bevie, what would you most like to leave to your children?" My first thought was, "Don't ask me; I'm too young to die! Why would you ask me such a question?"

I'm not ready to die yet, but neither was Don's mother. No one had ever asked me that question so directly before, and I couldn't think of a quick answer. This was on my mind the rest of the day, even as I drove home from shopping and even as I was preparing dinner. Finally, I answered the question to my own satisfaction, and I called her.

When I called Melba I said, "Melba, to answer your question, I would like my legacy to my family and my friends to be . . . love and laughter!" There was a silence and then a quiet "Thank you." I am afraid that I disappointed her! She was too young to realize how many times those two gifts would help her through the difficulties that come with living!

What would you want your legacy to your family to be? It goes without saying that you hope and pray that you have encouraged your children to love God and to go to Him with their problems. I am not sure I have succeeded, but I keep trying! I remember times of sorrow and times of happiness with my family. I loved my mother and father very much. My dad and I were very close and we had many long talks. We talked about God (Dad had studied to be a minister and I do not know why he changed his mind about the ministry or what discouraged him. He never said, and I respected him too much to ask), about life, about our dreams and family love! He was a wonderful man! Do you know, I cannot remember hearing him laugh very often. He smiled, and his smile was a beautiful thing, but I cannot remember hearing him laugh. He cared so much about everyone that he always carried a heavy burden.

Every life has its dark and its bright hours. Happiness comes from choosing which one you wish to remember. It is said you don't remember days, only moments. I have flashbacks of memory about certain events on certain days, but then I also have days that I remember in their entirety. Don't search for flaws in others as you remember. Instead, look for the love and the good things. You never can go back to live those hours over again. I block out the unhappy memories and regrets. You can ruin today by regretting yesterday. It won't change one thing. Living is for now! Start making your legacy now! Learn from the things you are sorry for and forget the hurts you may have suffered. That part of your life is over.

My dad's legacy to me was love for my fellow man. I love everyone, and I am interested in them. I truly am! I care for them, and I care about what happens to them. I wish I could bring them every happiness God gives us. Thank you, Dad! What was your legacy from your father?

I asked Roy about the "legacy of laughter," and his answer was, "Well, you can be content, happy and joyful without 'rolling in the aisles.'"

His answer made me "roll in the aisles," and it is true. You cannot leave contentment to your family, or joy, but you can pray for them. They make their own happiness with what life gives them, and this is aided by your gift of love and laughter. Love of God, laughter, and a sense of humor can help you weather many heavy storms.

Oscar Levant said, "Happiness isn't something you experience, it's something you remember." Do you believe that? I am not sure that I do! I believe that happiness is found along the way, not at the end of the road. To love and be loved is to feel the sunshine all around you! How blessed you are to have that sunshine in your life, even for a short time. Some people never know the meaning of true happiness because they don't take the time to enjoy it. That is truly sad.

I regret that I didn't take more time to tell my family how much they were loved or take the time to find the right words to tell them. I took it for granted that they knew, and, unfortunately, that is not always so. Suddenly, you find out that your children are grown, that they have their strengths and weaknesses, and you pray to God that you have given them courage, strength and determination to take whatever God has in mind for them with a smile and enjoy the times when they are blessed.

One of the happiest days of my life was an unexpected moment when my daughter told me that if her life ended right at that moment, that she had had a good life. Isn't that wonderful? She is her own woman now, and I don't think that I had a thing to do with it! She found her strength through adversity, and God has blessed her along the way with love and laughter.

I pray that you, too, are blessed and that you live and enjoy every happy moment and store it up for a rainy day!

Keep your sunshine hours a thing of beauty and create a legacy of love and laughter to your family from you. If you do that now, they will never lose you. You will be there in every smile and every laugh, and they will feel the sunshine all about them.

God Bless!

My Rose-Colored Glasses

Driving along the highway yesterday, I started listing (in my mind) my various faults and shortcomings. I seemed to have so many of them that it was really depressing—it had been that kind of a day! I started asking myself some very basic and honest questions and came quickly to the conclusion that I did not want to answer them honestly. I really don't want to know all of the things that are wrong with me. If I had to face the fact that all of the things people think are wrong with me really are true, I do not honestly think I could handle it!

In order to survive, one has to have some self-respect, some self-esteem, a reason for being, and a reason for living! I believe we are put on this earth for a special purpose, and God gives us basic qualities and talents if we will just use them, or at least try to find out what they are! Most of the time, I think we waste our God-given talents. My daughter wrote beautiful poetry and short stories when she was young, and perhaps she still does. I believe she wrote for her own enjoyment, but I wish she could have shared the beauty of her writing with the world. My grandson creates clever cartoons, but does not try to have them printed or accepted. He enjoys the creating! It is too difficult for a new young artist or author to be accepted. Those in charge never stop to think that the person without a broad education may be very intelligent and talented.

I am really enthused that the schools are now testing students. While I do not think that tests are infallible, it is probable that some children are not mechanically inclined or are musically tone deaf. It is also possible to be inept in one field without necessarily having a learning disability. The whole field of education is progressing and broadening its scope, as well as attitude, and I think it is wonderful that things are beginning to "happen," and I think it's about time! I do not think I have ever really accepted the premise that there are no fairy-tale scenarios, no guardian angels, no happy endings. Even though some members of my family think they have gone through life without happiness, they have had happy times and happy memories. I think everyone has some happiness in his or her life if he or she will take some special time or happening and examine it carefully for past pleasure and a bit of real joy. I always feel that tomorrow will be better and that "my day" will come!

I am very happy now! I have a beautiful life and, even though there are glitches now and then, I never dreamed that my life would be this wonderful. We always want something extra, don't we? We want a little more money, a little more pleasure, or a longer vacation! I always dream of the time that I can get my whole family together for a wonderful vacation. I see other families do this, but it seems that there is always something in our way, be it money, business, time, or their unwillingness to be together for a long period of time! I really do not know why we have not managed to do this, but I dream on!

I think that most people are to be trusted, that they are honest, that they care about their fellow man and that they are worth liking and getting to know better. I dream that I will find the "pot of gold" and be able to help everyone I know and love, and life will be perfect! I don't believe people are really greedy for money as much as they are afraid of what will happen to them and to their loved ones if they do not have it. Many lives have been lost due to the lack of money to care for illnesses or buy food for your family. There can be a great and terrible resentment in your heart for someone who has money to meet their problems when you do not have any. This can cause violence! I have been fortunate not to have been a witness to this type of problem, although there have been many times that I have wondered where the money was going to come from and how we were going to pay our many bills. These are problems that many people face at various times in their lives and if they haven't had those problems, then God has really blessed them!

At any rate, my "rose-colored glasses" keep me deeply loving my family and my friends, even if I do not accept the fact that they think I am rather dumb in not facing reality. I say wearing my "rose-colored glasses" is good because I like the "up" side of life!

Have you ever noticed people exchanging looks when you are speaking? Does this make you feel rather unnecessary? "Yes! Yes!" I say! I do not even think they realize that you can see them do this, so I can forgive! Wearing my "rose-colored glasses" again? You bet I am! I have traveled a long road that way, and I have been able (due to my glasses) to remain trusting, faithful, loving and happy. I really like it this way, and I thank God for giving me this trait. It has helped me considerably along life's way. I feel that I can always face tomorrow and whatever it may bring.

Would you like to try on my glasses sometime? They make the world as beautiful as it was intended to be. I really think you would like them, and they are free! You are welcome any time!

God Bless!

The Positive View

On my way to the doctor's office, I switched on my radio to listen to one of the talk shows. I always do this, seeking to broaden my mind, learn something, or be entertained. However, I usually become upset and angry! I wonder, then, if I am becoming intolerant, or perhaps more intolerant, to certain issues and expressed opinions. I learned long ago that there are many meanings and forms of "being smart"—book-smart, street-smart, macho-smart and on and on and on. None of these guarantee an answer for everything, or, perhaps I should say, a *correct* answer for everything.

When I listen to a talk show host or I ask a question, I only expect a different viewpoint. Much of the time, I listen to negative responses to questions or negative viewpoints on each and every topic. This distresses me terribly. It is an expression of the times. It is an expression of unhappiness, depression, hatred, or a dissatisfaction about everything! How sad! What a myopic indictment of the wonderful world we are going to pass on to our children. This seems to be an era of unhappiness with many marriages not working and with people complaining if they have to work hard enough to be tired at the end of the day. They say that you make more money on welfare if you aren't trained because wages are too low. They say that taxation for freedom is too high. They say that baby-sitters make too much money and they cannot afford to have an evening out. Single mothers complain because the fathers of their children only have to pay for support, while mommies have to come home from work and take care of them. Love is never mentioned, and caring and sharing is never mentioned. Employees say that their employers get all of the benefits and only share baseball tickets, et cetera, once in a while (was that mentioned as a part of their work package, I wonder?).

So you see, I have expressed a negative thought for everything that should be positive. The privilege of working and thanking God that you are able to work and the privilege and time to love, to share, to care and to say what you believe without fear are not even considered as reality at all!

The radio station I listened to today had an "expert" who seemed so very knowledgeable and who had facts and figures at his fingertips. He seemed so self-confident and so smart, but, as I listened to his answers and ideas for our country's problems and to his praises for other countries that, as he put it, "Know how to solve the world's problems if we would but listen" I could not decide which country he belonged to! I could hardly believe it when I discovered that he was an American. He criticized the United States for its foreign policy, welfare policy, medical expertise, and more. He even went back into history for his complaints, criticisms, and comments (he wasn't even living then, and so knew nothing of the feelings and emotions of the people to base those comments on, just cold facts and figures recorded somewhere in time). He attacked American educational policies, domestic problems, and he left nothing to be proud of, that is, if he could be believed.

I am sure we all agree that there is much to be improved upon, but if there wasn't we would have nothing to strive for, build upon, or plan for, would we? I guess I was really angry because I think that this country of ours is the best there is! If we don't like it, we can try to change it! Uniting in one cause (personal feelings aside) and working together solves a great many problems. There is no time for envy or discontent.

We should acknowledge that others have their own personal expertise in an area that we may know nothing of. We should accept that if a man has inherited money, it is because one of his ancestors worked for it! Each person is completely different and it will always be so! Will we spend our time wanting what someone else has? Will we spend our time being envious? Will we spend out time waiting for the world to come to us? Are we really so special that we deserve favors? We are all so different that we are bound to disagree, but being positive about it all and finding the sunshine in every day (even though we may have to struggle to find it) are big steps we all can take toward a better world and a better future.

How did we ever let money become the most important thing in our lives? Why and when did we decide that it was more pleasant to be negative than positive—or did we? I pray that we did not. If one person can make a difference in that attitude, I am here. My cup is not exactly running over, but it sure is not empty. It never will be with God to help me and the loving and sharing I have with my family plus the freedom I enjoy. I thank God for that freedom every day, and add to that a prayer of thanks for our veterans who were willing to give their lives for that freedom and for the men who put their lives and money on the line when they signed the Declaration of Independence.

We must work for a positive attitude and declare war on negativism. Many people will join us, share the positive and return our smile. Try it! You will find that we really need you in this world! We need you now! Step forward and form a new line of positivism. I will be the first to join you and, God willing, there will be many more of us as we go along!

God Bless!

The Gift of Laughter

I have to wonder if the gift of laughter is truly a gift, or if it is nourished and acquired through great effort on one's part! I have envied the turn of phrase of the humorist or comedian. I have a friend, Carol, who has a gift of repartee to be envied. Carol always sees humor in the smallest everyday occurrence. Once in a while, I find myself having a quiet laugh or two to myself as the day progresses. Whether or not I have a sense of humor on a particular day depends upon the day, the mood I am in, the mood of a loved one, or events and worries about everything and everybody.

The gift of laughter is a precious thing and I really believe that everyone has a certain amount of laughter in his or her make-up. I also believe that laughter has to be used and nurtured in order for it to become a natural part of everyday living. A person and his family are blessed if this is true in their world. Books could be written about this one subject because there are so many avenues of thought, including the necessity of laughter in everyday living.

When you get up in the morning, are you smiling, or are you sad? Think about this seriously! Then ask yourself this: "Am I in control of my mental and emotional attitude?" I feel that we definitely should be, even if we have to work at it. The person who has to worry about getting through each day does not have the time or the effort to meditate about mental and emotional attitudes. Some people must worry about where the money is coming from to pay bills, to buy food and to clothe their children. There are others who suffer great pain and pray for the strength to face each day and survive, never mind the smiling-face attitude. I offer the following advice from my heart and my love for you, not from the example I try to show to you!

When you arise in the morning, smile at your beloved, even if it is an effort to do so. You may be tired, have a headache, be depressed, but your smile will affect the whole day for each person you come into contact with. Remember this and start smiling the minute you get out of bed! Surprisingly enough you will immediately feel better yourself. Starting each day with a smile is the best medicine you can give to yourself and to others. A smiling face is a delightful gift. You have to feel good about yourself when you can make others happy. A cheerful laugh is so infectious you have to smile when you hear it. There are some you meet who never return your smile and sometimes even seem to resent you for it. They must be very unhappy and deserve your sympathy and understanding.

My children seem to remember the happy times in their growing-up years and I am happy for that. They talk and reminisce about the funny things and the happy things that happened. I have to feel good about that and I am proud that they have adjusted to life well enough that they can put the bad times away and go on with their lives.

Brooding about the past is a mistake that each one of us makes at one time or another. It is good to remember it if you intend to use the past to improve your future. But it is a mistake to use it to color the rest of your life. We do the best we can to cope with the life and the heritage we are given and mistakes are a part of the coping. God never intended that we should be perfect! There is really no such thing as perfection in this world; it isn't possible! Could a perfect person live in an imperfect world?

After all of these words are written, I still come up with the same solution. To be happy, you must laugh, smile and meet challenges with a sense of humor as well as hard work. Laughter is the music of the soul! Force yourself to laugh and to smile when things go wrong. It gets easier as you go along, and it is a beautiful habit to cultivate! I encourage you to try it on for size. You can't go wrong, and you will love it!

Go ahead and laugh! The world will laugh with you or perhaps even at you! But they will be laughing! It is a gift for you! Share it, nurture it, watch it grow, and make it a part of your heritage for your children and friends. Just laugh and see!

God Bless!

Daydreams

When I was a child, the world seemed to be such a wonderful place. It still is really, though I certainly have grown a great deal and hopefully, not only in size! I used to get out of bed at the first light and, though I cannot remember whether or not I ate anything, I do remember that I couldn't wait to get outside and climb my favorite tree. There, I would climb to the very tip-top and find my special nest of branches, seat myself very carefully and, after surveying the beautiful world from that great height, daydream.

I dreamed about becoming a beautiful princess in great detail. Dressed in beautiful colors (usually floor-length gowns), I would float gracefully down the stairs and glide around the dance floor while everyone watched me, for I was a wonderful dancer and quite famous! If there was a prince to dance with, he would be my dance partner. I was beautiful and kind, and everyone loved me.

I dreamed about all kinds of dancing. I was an acrobat (I believe they call them gymnasts today), a tap dancer, a ballerina, a toe dancer—I did it all! And I was the greatest dancer in the whole world. I didn't dream of applauding crowds but of how wonderful it would be to be able to do these things!

I dreamed of becoming another Shirley Temple but money didn't enter my mind. It was the wonderful act of dancing that was my dream. To be able to dance was the most exciting and wonderful world I could imagine!

The colors in my dreams were vibrant, exciting and alive! I couldn't draw a line with a pencil, but I never dreamed of that possibility anyway. Painting never entered my thoughts, even while I dreamed of beautiful and wonderful colors! I never in my wildest daydreams considered motherhood, family, or housekeeping. I did love to cook and begged mother to let me help. In my daydreams, I wrote beautiful poetry and wonderful books, and sad people became happy reading what I wrote for them. People all over the world invited me to come to their beautiful palaces and read the lovely things I wrote for them. I dreamed on and on about these things until I was called in for breakfast with the family.

And, now, in my golden years when my dreams of dancing are unreachable, I am writing! I am really sitting here writing! Who says that you cannot make your dreams come true? I danced and my friends thought that I was good, never wonderful, but doing something that they could not aspire to do. I wrote poetry but never even thought of trying to become published. I wrote philosophy in college and received "kudos" from my professors, but they never mentioned writing to me. They just complimented me upon my grasp of philosophy and the deeper meanings in the writings of famous men like Emerson, who was my favorite man (except for my dad, of course).

In retrospect I am one of the blessed people who, though never famous or successful financially, have during the years, made my daydreams come true! I have achieved for myself what I dreamed about when I was young—not success, but the doing of what I wanted to do!

I have many people to thank and remember along the way who made me feel that I could. There were, of course, many who were not interested in my dreams and still aren't, for they have their own. That is life, is it not? Perhaps they are busy making their own daydreams come true. I truly hope that they do. I wish I could help them! I wish that I could encourage them, and I will if they will only ask me!

God Bless!

A Day of Miracles

It was a beautiful day in August. The sun was shining, the sky was clear, and the baby was quiet having been fed, diapered and loved. Audrey was happily ironing. She was happy because life was good and she planned to finish her chores early in order to spend time chatting with her Aunt Hattie, who was visiting her mother. Her mother had promised to come by and tell her the plans they had made for the day. Living in a small town was such fun. They planned special things to do each day, and they enjoyed it all—the planning, the events, and the anticipating of sharing and enjoying with friends.

The telephone rang, and Audrey answered it on the second ring. "Audrey," said her mother, "this would be a perfect day to go to the Salem Reunion." This was a yearly event in the nearby town of Salem. The carnival came to town for a week and there was bingo, exciting rides, visiting with friends, picnics and outdoor dancing in the evening with a special orchestra.

"Mother, I am ironing, and I really don't think I should go today."

"But Audrey," sighed her mother, "Hattie would really like to go. She could see her old friends in Salem. And besides, Dad has the car, and you have that beautiful Maxwell that Glenn just bought. Please say you will go. Francis could drive and he would be so careful. We could visit all of the way there. I'll take care of the baby. Come on, honey, the ironing will wait until another day, or perhaps we can get home early enough for you to finish it."

"Well, okay, it does sound like such fun and I can be ready in a few minutes." What had started out to be a commonplace day had developed into a fun adventure. Audrey bustled around getting herself dressed and the baby tended to by packing extra diapers and such. She was thankful that Edythe, her three-year-old, was with her aunt on the farm. A few minutes later she heard her mother knock on the door.

"Hello! We're ready if you are," her mother said. "Can we help you carry things to the car? Here, I'll take the baby and put her with me in the back seat on this pillow."

And so, the big adventure began! Audrey, her six-year-old son, and Francis, her nephew, were in the front seat. Francis was driving. Her mother, Hattie (her aunt), and baby Beverly were in the back seat. Everyone was busy chatting away, as women are wont to do when they have a million stories to tell and family news to catch up on. It was a wonderful family day with so much love and pleasure filling the car. Everyone was in a festive, vacation sort of mood.

As they approached a railroad crossing which was at the top of the incline, Francis slowed the car so that he could look both ways (these crossings were very treacherous because the approaches were so steep). He saw nothing as he started up the sharp incline to the railroad tracks. The car stalled on the tracks because Francis did not shift gears just as a fast train rounded the curve.

Francis frantically tried to start the car but there was no time. Molly (Audrey's mother) picked up the pillow and the baby and started to throw her out of the window. As she did there was a huge crash followed by the sound of the locomotive grinding to a stop as its metal wheels screeched and screamed to a stop. Then nothing.

As the engineer climbed down from the cab of the engine, there was not a sound to be heard. There was a terrible and awesome silence as the summer heat beat down upon the lonely farmland. It was eerie and frightening! The engineer took one look at the mass of metal which had once been an automobile, and knelt down to look at the young man who had been thrown from it. He was unconscious but did not seem to be too badly injured.

Then he ran to the front of the locomotive, and there, caught on the cowcatcher, was the body of a young woman. She was breathing but obviously seriously injured. Help was needed immediately, and the engineer instructed a member of the crew to summon help on the double.

The engineer continued to search the area for the injured. He had no idea how many persons had been in the car. Ah, there was a boy! He knelt down to examine him, but heaved a big, heavy sigh as he found no sign of life. He rose to his feet to continue his search.

He went over to the car which was a jumbled mass of metal and looked through what once had been a window. "Oh, my god," he groaned, and turned away from the car for a moment as he tried to regain his composure and fight the urge to be violently ill. He stepped forward and looked into the car again. In the wreckage he could see at least one body, maybe more, with blood and severed limbs covering the inside of the vehicle. It was a sight which would haunt him forever.

Help finally arrived, and something could be done about the terrible wreckage that was once a car, the dead and the injured. After hours of sending the injured to the hospital and prying the dead, mangled bodies from what was left of the automobile, the automobile was identified as a 1920 Maxwell belonging to one Glenn S. Wade of Farina,

Illinois. Mr. Wade was notified by the Illinois Central Railroad representative and asked if he could tell them who was in the car and how many passengers there were.

I shall tell Glenn's story as it was related by him to me. I was the baby, Beverly, and Glenn was my father.

"I couldn't imagine why the Railroad would be calling me. But, you know, honey, I have always been psychic as far as my family is concerned and I felt that something was terribly wrong. I said, 'Glenn Wade speaking.'

"'Mr. Wade, do you own a 1920 Maxwell?'

"'Why, yes I do. Is there something wrong?'

"'I regret to inform you, sir, that there has been an accident and members of your family are in the hospital in Centralia. Can you come here right away and identify the injured parties?'

"'Yes, of course I can. I will be there as soon as I can. Can you tell me who is hurt and how badly?'

"'How many persons were in the car, Mr. Wade?'

"'There was my wife, Audrey, my six-year-old son, Winston Keith, my mother-in-law, Molly, her sister Hattie, and my nephew, Francis Schmidt and, of course, the baby.'

"'Baby? We found no baby! As far as the others are concerned, we have one young woman who is not expected to live, two older women who are deceased, and an older boy who has a badly mangled leg, superficial injuries and a few broken bones. There is a small boy who is deceased. We have no record of finding any baby. Of course we will send a search party back out there immediately. The clean-up crew is already out there working. It is terrible! Please come as soon as you can, Mr. Wade.'

"'I am on my way,' I said."

My dad then told me, "Honey, you can have no idea at all how devastated I was. I cannot describe it, and, unless you have been there, you cannot feel the sheer terror and disbelief that such a thing could happen! I hope that you never have to hear that you may have lost your entire family in one accident. I turned away from that telephone and began to shake so violently that I couldn't make my legs move. I couldn't think what I should do next. I knew that I had to get to my family as quickly as I could.

"'Glenn, Glenn, where are you?'" called my father-in-law as he came into the kitchen, letting the back door slam noisily behind him.

"'Please, God,' I prayed, 'help me find a way to tell him that his wife, Molly, is dead!' He adored Molly and often said that she made the sunshine in his heart and the love in his life. 'God,' I prayed, 'how can I tell him? Help me, oh Lord." This was stark reality! There was no bolt from the blue, no voice telling me what to say. I just stood there, frozen, unable to absorb what I had been told by the stranger on the telephone.

"My father-in-law was shaking me, saying 'Glenn, what is it, son? What is the matter with you, boy? You are as white as a ghost. Who was that on the telephone? Has something happened? Talk to me!'

"'Dad, there has been an accident. We have to go to the hospital in Centralia. Right now! There is no time to waste—we have to get there as soon as we can. I will tell you all that I know as we are driving. It is a forty-eight-mile drive and we will have to take your car—please hurry!'

"I don't remember getting in the car or anything. I finally told your granddad that I really did not know what had happened and that we would find out more of the details when we got to Centralia. It seemed to take forever to get there, and as I was driving, I seemed to hear the words, 'everyone is dead, everyone is gone,' over and over again. I felt as if I would go mad and that my life was over! I thought, 'God, how could you do this to me? Do I deserve this God? Please help me, oh Lord! Please help me!' and then—finally, we were there.

"I don't remember parking the car or getting out of it, but I rushed into the hospital with your granddad close behind me and grabbed the first person I saw.

"'Where is my family? I am Glenn Wade, where is my family?'

"'Mr. Wade, please follow me. There is someone here who wishes to speak to you. And you, sir,' she said to my grandfather, 'are you a member of the family?'

"'My wife was in the car,' my father-in-law said, 'and her sister, and my daughter—everyone I love was in that car!' And he started to tremble violently, taking hold of me to steady himself. 'Come on Glenn,' he said, 'let's go find out how bad things are. We can't find out anything just standing here, and Molly might need me. Don't just stand there. Let's go now!'

"So, we were told about the blind curve, the stalled car on the tracks, the engineer sounding the warning, the screeching of the wheels of the locomotive as he fought to stop in time, then, the terrible crash—the screams, the grinding metal, the smell of dust and oil and blood—then nothing, just a terrible stillness and silence! With the tears streaming down his face, the railroad representative said over and over, 'I am so sorry, I am so sorry, what can we do to help you? We are doing everything we can think of. I hate to ask it of you at such a difficult time, when you are suffering such shock and sorrow, but we need to ask you to identify the victims of the accident. There is no one else to ask! Will you please come this way?'

"Your granddad and I stumbled along behind this man, this stranger, who had told us such a terrible and unbelievable thing. Surely he had to be wrong! This could not be happening! But it was! We entered a room which seemed to be filled with bodies—the bodies of the ones we loved."

Dad continued his story in a quiet hushed voice, even now finding it difficult to speak of this tragic time in his life. "As we stood in the silent room, we couldn't comprehend the terrible things we were seeing—there was your grand-dad's cherished Molly in bits and pieces, and Hattie, her beloved sister, with her body in two pieces. Over to one side, a small boy whose body seemed intact, but whose head was crushed. It was all so terrible that my mind could not accept what I was seeing. It was so horrible that your granddad became violently ill and I had to stand strong and take over for both of us.

"How can I describe it to you, Bevie? There are no words to tell you how we felt. The horror, the grief, the terrible grisly details, and over all of this, the disbelief that such a tragedy could happen! Not to us! All I can do is to try to tell you what I remember. I was in such a state of shock that I am sure that I have forgotten things even though it all seems to be permanently etched in my brain. When I close my eyes, I can still see things so clearly even though it happened about thirty years ago. Molly was dead! Hattie, Molly's sister was dead! Francis, our nephew, who was driving had a broken collar bone. Though I am not sure, I believe he also had a broken arm and a broken leg. Your brother, Winston Keith, was in with the dead until your Aunt Carrie, Francis' mother, insisted that they 'clean him up.'

"Two dedicated young interns found a faint heartbeat and tried out the new concept of artificial respiration. It was truly a miracle! Keith started breathing on his own, not strongly, but he was breathing. There was not a spot on his head that wasn't cracked like an egg and no one ever though he would live. But the young doctors would not give up. They put a metal plate in his head, bandaged what needed to be bandaged, and took over his care themselves. They were determined to save this little boy if at all possible, and he lived! Thank the Lord!

"Audrey, your mother, had been terribly injured. She was dragged along the cindered railroad tracks and the cinders cut into her knees, her shoulders and her head. She was cut and bruised all over her body. The doctors told us to pray that she would make it and believe me, we did just that!

"Then there was the baby! That baby was you, Bevie. When we arrived at the hospital, there was no baby! There was not even the knowledge that there had been a baby in the car. Even as I asked about you, the railroad crew was at the site of the accident, clearing away the debris, the mass of metal that had been the Maxwell and cleaning up all visible signs of the accident. As far as anyone knew, the baby had not been found!"

Dad continued his story. "As I was sitting by your mother's bedside holding her hand, she was still unconscious. My mind kept going over and over the terrible day. It seemed as if we had been in this hospital forever. Audrey's father had become terribly quiet, doing what had to be done, notifying relatives, calling Hattie's family, making funeral arrangements, et cetera. He told his other two daughters that they could not view the remains of the terrible wreck because their sister could not be there with them and she might not live to even be told that her mother was dead.

"As I sat there praying for my loved ones to live and praying that my baby daughter would be found and that she would be found alive, a sense of peace came over me, and I felt certain that the Lord was with me.

"As I prayed, 'Thy will be done, Lord, help me, Oh Lord, give me the strength to accept Thy will, oh Lord,' a nurse ran into the room crying, 'Oh Mr. Wade! Mr. Wade! They have found the baby, Mr. Wade! They have found her and she's alive!'

"I rushed into the corridor where I met the doctor as he was starting to open the door, and he was holding you, Bevie. Thank God! I took you into my arms and held you close to my heart. I just stood there holding this warm bundle, the tears rolling down my cheeks and I know that I will never forget the warm surge of love I felt. I hurt with it, for I loved you so much and God was so good!

"'Where did they find her?' I asked. 'Would you believe me if I told you that when the crew was cleaning up the wreckage, someone saw the back seat of the car out in the farmer's cornfield. When they went out to pick it up, they found your baby under it. The impact of the train as it hit your car must have thrown the seat out in the field and the women holding the baby must been trying to throw her out the window. It is amazing! Truly a miracle! She will be fine. Her little skull is cracked all the way around, but she is so young and her bones are so soft, she will heal rapidly. Six-month-old babies do heal quickly, and we are fortunate to have a young mother next door to the hospital who will be able to nurse her. She is what we call a wet nurse.'"

My dad, who was a deeply religious man, concluded this incredible and shocking story of great tragedy for our family as he said, "I thank God every day for my blessings, and as I look back upon that terrible day, I realize that along with its tragedies, it was also a day of many miracles. My son lived for thirty more years. There were some side effects from his terrible injury, but his brain was not damaged, and God had given him a beautiful musical talent to share with others. My wife and companion is still with me. And you, well, you are very special to me. I feel that you were my own very special miracle. When the world looked so bleak and the future so uncertain, you were given back to me by God as a light in that darkness. You were a sign that He was with me and that everything would be as it should be. I thank God for you every day. You are my very own special miracle and I love you. You will always be Daddy's baby!"

God Bless!

Beautiful Christmas

Christmas is the time of gifts and love and miracles. It is a time for sharing with others what we are so fortunate to have. Gifts are tied with heart strings attached, and he who has no Christmas in his heart will never find Christmas under a tree. If the heart is not involved, Christmas is an empty season. It is the way you spend Christmas that makes it far more important than how much you spend. God gives us things to use and people to love and enjoy. Let us not spend Christmas but keep Christmas in all of its loveliness and tradition of sharing the miracle of God. May we keep it in our hearts always.

Most everyone says, "Wouldn't it be nice to have the Christmas spirit all year long?" Yes, as a matter of fact, it would! Do you think that there would be the danger of growing careless and bored? I feel that we must bear our share of sorrow, the pain of growing, and the learning of how to share. Some people are the givers and some are the takers. However, through the Christmas miracle of Jesus' birth and the glow of that magic time, everyone learns to give and to share. There is the warm feeling of satisfaction when you give something special, with special thoughtfulness and lots of love. Don't you find this to be true?

There is the special gift that God sends to people who are lonely, afraid, crippled or ill. He gives them Himself if they will only believe that He is with them always. What a miracle we have in Jesus! We should try to share that miracle with everyone we know with Christmas cards, gifts, Christmas stockings stuffed for the poor and that special gift for a child who needs love and material gifts to prove that they are not forgotten. A gift is a sign that Jesus lives and that Santa is here at this special time!

As we travel through our life, we are blessed to have the Lord with us to keep our thoughts pure, our hearts kind, and to help us during our difficult times. He helps us to keep the spirit of youth, enthusiasm, love and sharing alive; always looking to the future and whatever it will bring. We share that love with one another as I write these words and you read them. Aren't we blessed to have each other and Christmas?

God Bless!

Christmas Visit

I thought you might like to share some of my very special Christmas memories.

When I was a little girl, every happening, it seemed to me, was used as an example of what to do and how to do it in a like situation. Good manners were a must at home as well as when in company. The Golden Rule was referred to at least once a day, and, more importantly, we were taught by example to care for and share with others. Love was an essential part of our very being. At Christmas time we filled stockings at church and helped mother fill baskets for the less fortunate. Oh yes, we knew who they were, for we lived in a very small town, and we tried to take care of our own. The great "white fathers" in Washington were busy running the country, and only those without food, without family, and without a home, were given help or care by the state or county governments. We were a closely knit community, and I was so blessed to be a part of that kind of life.

When I was grown, living in the suburbs of the city, enjoying my life and thanking God for everything good in my world and asking for His help for the "not so good" things, Christmas was even more special to me. I was all ready for Christmas one year. I was going to relax and feel proud of myself, for everything had been done.

Have you ever had the feeling that there is something you have left undone that is very important? Well, there I was, all ready for the holiday; the Christmas cards had all been addressed, special notes written to those special people and mailed. The gifts were all wrapped and under the tree, and the gifts for the "angel tree" at church had been delivered.

Yes, I felt proud of myself. Besides, the Visa and MasterCard bills would not have arrived until the next year! And yet, I had this nagging feeling. As I sat there, glancing once again at the Christmas cards we had already received, I suddenly knew what it was!

This very special couple, friends of mine, had no family to spend Christmas with, and they were not too well. I had promised to stop by to see them before my family arrived and before I found myself with no time. That very week I had received a card and note from them, inviting me to stop in if I wasn't too busy. "We know how busy you are," Alice had written.

How could I have forgotten? And I knew as soon as I thought that, that I really hadn't forgotten at all. I did not want to go. It was not the age difference that made it so difficult to find a common ground for conversation, but we just didn't have anything in common any more. We had grown apart in so many ways and that was really sad because I really loved her.

Alice was no longer able to attend the same patriotic meetings that we used to attend together, as we served on the executive board together and believed in the same things with the same "love of country, love of God, and love of our fellow man." Hank was no longer able to drive Alice to all of those meetings and wait for her. He was such a sweet man and loved his Alice so! She returned that love. Every other word was, "Hank says" or "Hank likes" or

"Hank is so wonderful" and "he does so much for me and I worry about him working so hard."

They were very special people and I had wanted to remember them that way. I didn't want to visit them just because I felt that it was my duty! I hated myself for feeling that way and I never would forgive myself if I didn't see them during the holidays. I really had no excuse! I might as well have gone right then and gotten it over with.

I put on my warm hat and gloves, and, taking the street guide just in case I got lost, I started on my way. It wasn't necessary to call Alice because they were at home most of the time now. Oh, how I dreaded that trip! Finally I arrived at their house. I went slowly up the walk and then I was there! There was nothing else to do, except ring the doorbell and so I did. I heard nothing. I rang the bell again. Still nothing. The third time, I decided that I might as well leave. They were probably taking a nap.

But then, I heard the china rattle on the hutch as someone came down the hall. There was a struggle with the door as it popped open, and there was Alice! Her eyes lit up with surprise. "Come in, come in" she laughed as she took my hand and pulled me into the house and into the parlor. All of a sudden, I smelled the spiced oranges, the pine of the tree, and the smell of baking cookies. I felt six years old again. My thoughts ran hither and thither, dancing among the old family ornaments, and my eyes noticed the old wooden soldiers lined up in a row.

"Sit down, sit down. I'll call Hank," she said, and I sat down and started to chatter nervously about the weather, the flu, the traffic, and this, and that, and nothing important. Then Alice touched my hand and softly said, "What's new with you, Bev?"

Well, what a visit we had. We talked about old times, my family, her illness, the future, everything . . . and it was wonderful! How glad I was that I had gone!

"Just a minute," she said, "I'll call Hank and fix a cup of tea. Just you sit there, I will be right back." As I looked around the parlor, my eyes filled with tears as I recognized the lovely porcelain nativity set and the beautiful crystal. The old Christmas cards were on display, and there was the special place where the cards from old friends were displayed. How beautiful memories are! The room glowed with love and memories. Not self pity but lots and lots of love and warmth and closeness and happiness flowed in the room—laughter remembered!

Alice and Hank appeared with smiles on their faces, and we sat down to enjoy our cup of tea. I realized, then, that I had been blessed with a very special day. I had witnessed a triumph over illness and pain, a loving togetherness that nothing could destroy—not illness, not old age, nothing. It was a miracle of the triumph of two loving people who treasured their time together!

Thank you, God, for allowing me to share that special love and companionship. No loneliness or depression or defeat—just a joy to behold, this beautiful love. Oh Lord, for this gift of allowing me to share that special moment, I thank you!

God Bless!

Memories of World War II

It is very difficult for me to find a way to relate what effect the war had upon the young people living during World War II. I can only speak from personal experience. There are those, I am sure, who would disagree with me completely. I was a young girl from a small town, happily married to a young man from the suburbs of Saint Louis. We were carefree but because of the Depression years while we were growing up, we knew how to budget our money and make a dollar stretch while trying to live life to the fullest.

Ed, my first husband, was a happy sort of fellow with a ready smile, and we adored each other. We lived in a small house in Brentwood, a small suburb of St. Louis. It was a very inexpensive home which suited our needs and one which we could afford. They call them starter homes today, I believe! We paid the large sum of $25 per month for our mortgage which included taxes and insurance. We were very much aware of the rumblings of the war and what was going on in Europe, but it seemed very far away from us as we lived each day to the fullest—enjoying our friendship with our neighbors, making new friends and getting to know one another better every day.

We had rented our little house. I had joined my husband in Marion, Illinois, where he was working on the veteran's hospital there for his father. I hated it there—I guess because I was so lonely. We decided that we should either start a family, or I should go to work. Starting a family won, and we were very fortunate for I became pregnant right away.

We were so thrilled! We were getting ready to move back to our home in Brentwood and life seemed perfect. Then one Sunday morning as we listened to the radio, we heard the news about Pearl Harbor. We couldn't believe our ears! It had to be some sort of a nightmare!

Ed was so stunned and angry, he was ready to enlist at once and only my pregnancy stopped him. I really felt guilty for being the cause of his staying at home, and yet, was glad that he did not go. Some of his friends enlisted anyway, leaving their children and wives at home with their parents. I cannot begin to tell you about the atmosphere at home, at work, in the stores and on the streets. The little black cloud did not go away and we listened to the radio, read the papers avidly, trying to keep up to date with what was going on in Europe and in the Pacific. Remember, there was no television then.

By this time, we had a beautiful baby girl, whom we adored! I thanked God that she was healthy and that her Daddy was home with us. Six months later, I discovered that I was pregnant again! I wanted this baby, but was scared to death. Yes, scared, because her Daddy had received his draft notice, and I wanted him to be at home when she was born. Ed was working on "war related jobs" but because he was an officer in his father's company, he was not considered necessary to the war effort. I will never forget the day that the Government notified us that Scullin Steel (a job on which Ed was working) had asked the government for a postponement of induction so that he could finish their work. Thank God, a reprieve!

The months went by! January 22, 1944, Judith was born. When her Daddy visited me in the hospital he said, "You may now salute me. I have joined the navy! Uncle Sam gave me a choice—the army or the navy."

My heart seemed to stop beating. I couldn't believe this could happen to me. It was all a part of what was going on for so many young people. The day my little girls and I went to Union Station to see Ed leave was the day that I finally realized that the war was now a part of my life. It was the day that I realized that real life is not always a storybook and that I was responsible for the lives of two little girls, one sixteen-month-old, and one one-month-old.

I was frightened of the responsibility of my girls, of being alone, of something happening to Ed and plain afraid that I might not be able to cope with it all. As I write this, I can almost hear my girls telling me, "Mother, don't be dramatic," but I must tell you, those were dramatic times! Friends and relatives were being killed, captured and tortured every day!

It was so hard to be at home and not know what was really happening. Ed had devised a way for me to know where he was when he left for the Pacific. We bought two maps of the Pacific and they were just alike. We fit the map over the stationery, just so, and when Ed wrote to me, he would stick a pin through the stationery at the spot where he was. When I received the letter, I put the pin through the hole in the paper and stuck it through onto the map, and I knew where he was, at least approximately. He was on a floating dry dock. I believe it was the ABSD7. These were strange ships in that they could go down into the water somewhat like a submarine, float a damaged ship onto it's deck, and raise the ship up out of the water for repair at sea. Quite remarkable really. I had been fortunate enough to be invited by the tow boat captain's wife to visit the ship before it left the country. This floating dry dock had no power to move the ship. It had to be towed or pushed to its destination by ocean-going tugs. They had no power and no protection from the enemy, so they were sitting ducks.

Yes, I was frightened! I was so afraid that one of my babies would need me in the night and I would not hear them. I truly believe that I spent my sleeping hours with one ear awake for sounds of my babies. I was proud that my husband was serving his country, but I was so lonesome. He was the only man on our street to be in the service and on the weekends, everyone went somewhere with their families, and the girls and I were all alone. My friend next door was my buddy, but even she would say, "I am not going to give you any sympathy." She meant well. She didn't want me to fall apart. But what she, nor anyone else realized, was that I needed someone to hold me in their arms and tell me that they could understand how much I needed love and understanding. I needed someone to share some of my fears and tell me that everything was going to be all right. It was hard to be brave, capable, strong and all of those good-sounding things, when inside you were crying for so many things.

My mother-in-law and father-in-law dutifully came over about once a month with ice cream to visit the girls and me for about an hour. This was nice, but I spent the hour hearing about how much Dad K missed his son and that it was all right for me because I was young, and no one realized how hard it was for him. Now that I can look back on those times, I wonder if I gave him what he needed. Perhaps he was crying inside like I was!

Ed let me know that they were headed to Corrigidor and that I wouldn't hear from him for a while. I knew what that meant. When he left for the Pacific, I did not hear from him for over forty-five days. Don't forget that his ship was being towed and that they were sitting ducks for the submarines. The news informed us about storms in Corrigidor, about the men being killed there, and MacArthur promising to return. I still had not heard a word from Ed. Had he been captured or killed? Where was his ship? There was no news at all! As I said, these were dramatic times.

People were sorry for me, but I had too much pride to moan and groan about my lot. I was supposed to be brave and I was going to be—no matter what! Life does go on, and they had their own lives to lead.

Sometimes some of my friends (I had only been there long enough to make a few) and I would play bridge. They were living at home and so they came to my home because I couldn't afford a baby-sitter, even when one was available. When I went to their houses, I took my girls along and put them to bed while I played bridge and visited. They were so good. God was blessing me. They woke up smiling when I picked them up in the middle of the night, told everyone good-bye, and then we went home to an empty house. But it was more than a house; it was a home filled with love and prayer and thankfulness for each day. There were good days and some that were not at all good! I was always happy with my girls and thanked God for them every day.

The days went by so slowly. I waited each day for the postman. He was so very nice! He would ring the doorbell and say brightly, "No mail today, but there is sure to be some tomorrow. Now you just sit down and write him a nice long letter, and you will feel better." I would do just that. We were told not to write anything but good news and nice things, so I wrote about the cute little things that the girls did, what they would say, etc. This was good therapy for me, too, for I had no one else to share their "growing up" days with. Your children are only super special to you. I learned that in a hurry!

I don't remember feeling sorry for myself. I was too busy keeping up a good front, and being the brave mother. I honestly don't think I felt sorry for myself until it was all over and Ed was back home. I knew that he was alive and when he was coming home. He hadn't gone to Corrigidor after all because of the earthquake and storms. He told me what ship he was on and when he would arrive in San Francisco and that he would call me.

He was in the Pacific until the war was over. The day the war ended, I took my scrub bucket with ice and champagne in it, my two girls and a blanket, went outside and sat on my front lawn and toasted the end of the war! One by one, my neighbors joined me with their buckets of iced champagne and it turned out to be quite a celebration as we laughed for the living and the boys coming home, cried for the ones who would never come home. We laughed in relief that it was over and cried for the joy of it! How can I tell you how I felt?

I couldn't believe it was over and that Ed would be coming home. I didn't realize how much I had changed and matured and I did not realize how changed Ed would be. I thought everything would be just like it was when he left. You can never go back, can you? He was never the same carefree boy that I married. He wasn't well, but he loved the navy and didn't really want to come home and work in an office. He did not really want a self-sufficient, rather bossy wife who was used to calling the shots for her family. But try as I might, I couldn't become the naive green girl that he married. Life, war, babies, grief for lost friends and relatives—growing up—had changed all of that forever. One could only thank God for life and health and the chance to go forward with a beloved family. The war was over!

God Bless!

School Reunion

When I attended a school reunion recently, I had many adjustments to make when we gathered together. How did everyone get so old when I am so young? I loved everyone that was there, and I didn't care how old they were for they were my childhood friends, and therefore, very special to me.

I believe the biggest adjustment I had to make with my friends was that we had all grown with the passing of the years and everyone had grown in a different way. This was, of course, because we all had led different lives after leaving the cocoon of a small town and our families. I thought that we would all still hold the same basic viewpoints, the same religious beliefs, and of course, the same moral standards that had been such a major part of our lives.

I was wrong!

Life changes us, I believe, not the years. When I was a little girl, I found it shocking when people told lies, stole small things from the local department store, talked back to their mommies and daddies, threw tantrums in public and generally misbehaved in public or in front of company. Do you know, I still feel that way!

My old friends don't agree with me. They call this "mellowing." Do I agree with them? Not really! I must admit that becoming more tolerant with the years is most attractive in everyone, but when does tolerance and mellowing become being permissive? How does it happen to a person who has been reared to adhere to certain standards? I cannot answer that because I did not live in the same home that they did, nor did I have the same parents.

We are now in an era where skeletons are coming out of the closets by the hundreds, maybe thousands! It has become the "in" thing to talk about your parents and the traumas they have caused in your life; or the sex abuse from a relative or a neighbor or a trusted baby-sitter. People who would never ever utter a swear word or tell a risqué story will openly talk to acquaintances or the press about sex abuse. I would suppose that this is much more healthy than to hide it away in the closet, but sometimes it seems that everyone must get on the bandwagon and tell all! To what purpose?

I really do not know what to think when I hear attorneys defend murderers using the excuses of sexual, emotional or physical abuse when they were young. If this is a good excuse, then would not everyone be excused for any misdoing? I am sure we can all find some time in our life when we felt misunderstood, or were punished for something that we didn't do. On the other hand, I also feel sure that there was some time in your life when you got by with something you should have been punished for. This is a part of living!

My second big shock at this reunion was to find that even though my friends and I remembered the same incident, we each remembered it in a different way. We were sitting in my hotel room having refreshments of various kinds and reminiscing about our grade school days. We agreed about the big things like the play "Tom Thumb's Wedding" in which many of us took part, and the girl who "got pregnant" in her second year of high school. However, we each had a different girl in mind and never did resolve the identity of the poor girl! But then it does not matter now, does it? We were not faced with how to handle the situation at school. In those days, the unfortunate young lady was quietly asked to leave school so that the innocents would not be faced with an unpleasant fact of life.

We violently disagreed about the small incidents like who stuffed the grasshoppers into their socks at recess in order to let them out during the exam and cause a big hoo-rah, and who really tipped over the outhouse with Mr. So-and-so inside, and who really planned and executed the wonderful private dance parties that we all went to and remember with such delight, and even who belonged to the Ladies Reading Circle. No one was allowed to join this exalted group unless she was a female descendent of a Charter member. I still have a silver spoon which was given to me by the group when I was married, and I treasure it. That group is no longer in existence, but remembering the teas and special dinner parties were an important part of my childhood.

We even differed about best friends and who they were. Some of us claimed the same best friend. The most vocal person usually won, leaving the others rather at a loss! Am I remembering this wrong? Was I misled?

There were special events, some of which I thought were highlights of my growing up, that some of my friends didn't remember at all. I thought they were never to be forgotten! Wonders!

Some of the special things were the important people in our lives and none of us had forgotten them! Some were very special to each one of us. I remember my sixth and seventh grade teacher, Miss Alice Readnour. I was intimidated by her even while I really liked her. I learned more under that teacher than any other teacher I ever had. Even my college teachers were not able to transmit the desire to learn like she did. I hope that wherever she is, she knows how much I liked and admired her. She is one of the caring people that you read about who give up their plans of marriage and children to keep on working and caring full time for an invalid mother. Today, nursing homes and retirement centers do all of that, but it really was so much nicer to have them at home. Some of my friends still do that, for their mothers are too important for anyone else to care for.

I remember friends who were so restricted by their parents that even then, in what the young folk call the old days, we wondered why they didn't revolt. But how could they? There was no place to run to! There were no street people and no havens for those who ran away from home. Am I saying that these things are wrong? Not really! Just different! So many things seem better, but sometimes I wonder if the ideas are taken over by people who need a cause and who have had no first-hand experience! The idea is terrific, but perhaps carried too far and to an extreme. The middle of the road policy is not always wrong!

Then we remembered the pranks we pulled. Funny how so many of us thought it was someone else's idea when things went wrong and took the credit when it was just fun! Like the outhouse story I mentioned.

We all agreed about one special lady in our lives! Nettie Sapp Wheeler had moved back home from New York city and loved advising and chaperoning the young people of our town. Our parents didn't worry about us when we went to her home for the evening. We played cards, went on scavenger hunts and played charades. I'm afraid I have forgotten some of the fun games we played but we always had a wonderful time! She listened to our problems, suggested solutions, but advised parental guidance. She really cared about us, and we knew it! We really loved and trusted her. She was forever young! And we are forever blessed to have known her!

We will plan another reunion because we had a wonderful time at this school reunion. I heartily recommend it. It encompasses so many ages and covers so many special, past years. Get together with your old friends and see if their memories match your memories. Let me know if they ever do!

God Bless!

Strength Through Courage
Courage Through Strength

I can go back through generations on my mother's side of the family and find many women of great strength! In the telling, they were women of rare courage; they were survivors and women of determination! I find myself thinking of these women at the oddest moments, realizing that though my memory and the stories told to me are rather incomplete, the stories told were a saga of very strong women. I have to wonder then, was it circumstance that made them strong? Were they women of courage, women of strength or a combination of both? They were survivors! What was it in their character that made them as they were? The following stories are true ones and I have limited them to three generations starting with my mother. You can decide what you feel made them strong and then I shall tell you what I have decided!

The Strength of Mom Audie

Audrey was a very headstrong and spoiled young woman! Being the youngest of three girls, beautiful, creative and indulged, she was the most popular girl in her class in school. She lived in an age where decorum was a must and good manners were taken for granted. Growing up in a small village made civil behavior something that was taken for granted unless you were a young man. Then you were expected to sow a few wild oats as you matured. Even those wild oats were expected to be sown with good taste, and the young ladies of your social group were always to be held in the highest regard.

My father, Glenn, was a gentle, young man—a dreamer, extremely well-read and with the desire to become a minister. He had been moved around a great deal during his growing-up years because his mother had died when he was nine years old. He was reared for a time by his grandmother and then lived with his father and new stepmother when he was in his early teens. Glenn had two sisters and one half-sister and he adored all three of them. His two sisters were parceled out with relatives when their mother died, but unlike Glenn, they were reared in one home. Glenn was moved around a great deal and, being a male, everyone felt that was perfectly all right for him!

For several years Glenn lived with Audrey's family because he was apprenticed to her father to learn the trade of cabinet maker. Glenn and Audrey fell in love—or at least they thought they had. Audrey's parents were fond of Glenn, but felt that Audrey was too young to even consider love and marriage! She was only seventeen.

Seemingly, Audrey accepted the verdict that she was too young and life proceeded normally. Then Audrey convinced her parents that it might be a good idea for her to attend the Catholic convent for her senior year studies. Although they were not of the Catholic faith, several of Audrey's closest friends were going to go to school there. Her parents felt that this might help keep the romance in abeyance as it was beginning to look rather serious between the two young people.

Audrey went away to school and Audrey and Glenn traded many letters keeping the post office busy. One weekend, Glenn went out of town and—you guessed it—Audrey and Glenn eloped! The family accepted the fact as gracefully as possible. What else could they do? The first blow came for Audrey when a party was given for the newlyweds, and naturally, she wanted something new to wear. As was her usual practice, she went to the store, bought the material and the pattern, cut out a blouse and stopped by to see her mother.

"Mother, I need to have this blouse for the party tomorrow night. Shall I put it on the sewing machine for you? I am so excited, won't it be beautiful?"

"I am sorry, Audrey," said her mother, "but you are a married lady now and you will have to sew your own clothes."

Audrey cried, stamped her foot, cried some more, but to no avail. Her mother refused to discuss it. Audrey, being a stubborn girl, went home determined to make the blouse herself. She was going to wear the new blouse to the party, no matter what! Well, I do not know how many times she sewed, ripped out the stitches, sewed some more, cried, then ripped out stitches, and sewed some more. Do I need to tell you that she wore the new blouse to the party, and it was perfectly beautiful? The years went by. There were some bad times, but all in all, they were happy years.

Glenn was now the postmaster, member of various men's clubs and on the school board, and there were three children, a son and two daughters. Audrey was a good mother, strict in regard to obedience, good manners and proper things to do. She taught all three of her children to cook, clean, iron and do whatever necessary to have a well-organized home to be proud of. Her children were going to know how to do things when they married!

The years passed, as they inevitably do, and then came the Great Depression. Because of Glenn's position, the Depression years didn't really become frightening for them. Audrey kept a pot of soup on the stove all of the time for she never knew when Glenn might send someone home for something to eat. Sometimes they asked for odd jobs to pay for their hot dinner and sometimes not, but the food was always there for anyone who was hungry.

One young man insisted on working for his dinner. He was so pale and thin and obviously not well, and Mother felt so sorry for him that she packed a hearty parcel of food for him to take along with him when he left. Years later he returned to our home in a beautiful limousine to thank Mother and Dad for literally "saving my life" and giving him the faith to continue the fight to survive!

The depression in our family came when the administration changed in Washington. You see, the President always signed the Certificate for the Postmaster and if no one requested the position when a new president was elected, the same man continued in his same position. When the administration changed, one of the men my dad had employed and had taught the job requested the position. Since, thanks to Dad, he was highly qualified, my father was asked to resign his position and that is when our depression began. That in itself, is another story.

Mother was magnificent, encouraging Dad to do things like applying for specialized positions that only he was qualified for in the state of Illinois and standing for election to a political office in the county. Most importantly, she did not complain about her lack of material things or the fact that she had to scrounge and to budget in order to keep her family comfortable. Of course, it must have hurt to have to tell her youngest (me) that there would be no more dancing lessons, but she always took the positive side.

"Look what wonderful things you have had the opportunity to learn. You can always laugh and dance and sing and no one can take that from you." When it was time to go to college, she said to me when I told her how badly I wanted to go, "Of course you can go to college if you want to badly enough! You can always find a way—just get busy and find out what scholarships are available and what you have to do to get one. When you have done that, then we will visit the college and you can find a job to pay for your room and board. There is nothing you cannot do if you want to badly enough."

Imagine hearing this positive and wonderful advice from a young woman who had been spoiled at home, married at a young eighteen years and babied by the husband who adored her. Everyone always had said that Mother never had to grow up because everyone spoiled her! Perhaps these were her growing-up years. I cannot say and she is no longer here to tell me. Suffice it to say, she met her problems and handled them wisely and cheerfully! I call that strength, don't you?

Those were very difficult years, both economically and emotionally. My dad had such faith in his fellow man and always said, "My friends will help me if I ever need it." But they were not there when the time of need came. Mother kept a happy face, an encouraging attitude and everyone survived and became stronger and better human beings. And, yes, I did go to college, thanks to Mother! Where did her strength come from? Was it faith, circumstance, survival instincts or heritage? It was all of these plus lots and lots of love—love for her family and love from her family. I am so proud and so blessed that she was my mother! Some of my strength must have come from her. Thank you, Mom!

God Bless!

Beverly

I know I will sound prejudiced in finding words to describe my firstborn. Of course, I am prejudiced! I adore both of my beautiful daughters and will fight for them to the death. At the same time, I can recognize that no one is perfect even though I feel that mine are the exception.

Beverly, Bee Sue as she was called when she was small, was one of those rare children who go through their growing up years causing no worries or problems. She was a bright, sunny, happy child and very caring and loving with a smile for everyone she met. She was interested in everybody and everything and when her baby sister, Judith, was born, delighted in being the mother's helper, the bottle carrier and the big sister! Their father was fighting the "war to end all wars" in the Pacific and Bee Sue talked to her sister all of the time about "Our daddy who is in the navy" and sang "Bell-bottom trousers, coats of navy blue, I love a sailor and he loves me, too" to her over and over.

I do not want to give the impression that Bee Sue was a goody two-shoes because she definitely was not. She was a beautiful child with a very sweet disposition but with a mind of her own! I recall the time when she was learning to ride her two-wheeler bike. I had balanced her for a while until I felt that the time had come for her to try it on her own. I watched her from the bedroom window. She would get on the bike, go across the drive onto the lawn, hit a tree (the only one there), fall off, cry, pick up the bike, go back onto the driveway and start over again with the same result. I can't tell you how many times she kept trying. I was sitting at the window crying with her but proud of her determination. Finally, just when I had decided that I couldn't stand it any longer, she mastered the thing. Yes, really, she could ride the bike like a veteran and she was so proud! Believe me, so was I! This determination has been a godsend to her through all of her life.

Bee Sue had average grades in school unlike her sister, Judy, to whom book-learning was easy! We lived in St. Louis County during the war, the Lake of the Ozarks (another story) for five years and then back in St. Louis. Bee Sue adapted well to the moves, but Judy had a difficult time. I don't know what she would have done without her big sister. Bee would take her by the hand and off they would go. She would try to smooth the way for her sister, fighting her battles for her, encouraging her, and loving her! They had a wonderful relationship with the usual spats now and then, but not often; and a loyalty to one another that was beautiful to see!

Bev (her nickname as she matured) finished school in Ladue and went to college, majoring in physical education. She was a natural in sports, and her attitude in school sports had always been one of determination to win! She was the smallest in her class, but made up for that with spunk, speed and that determination. She is still that way today! Thank God!

When she finished college, she spent the summer in Norway with a group of thirty students who were representing their countries. She loved it! Then she came home to work! She taught physical education and health class in a rather small town. Everyone liked this lovely young teacher who entered into every event with enthusiasm and goodwill. It was inevitable that eventually she would meet the eligible young bachelor around town, and, you guessed it, they fell madly in love! Art was a farmer from a long line of farmers and so Bev became a farmer's wife, and learned to drive tractors and plow a straight line, but she drew a line at raising chickens.

Bev still taught school. She was a very strict teacher, but her students loved her and they learned extra things like manners, cleanliness, sportsmanship, discipline and how to play the ukulele and sing together. She also took them on hayrides on the farm, ice skating on the pond and had wiener roasts. Art learned that there was much more to life than just farming, and they were very happy together. They had a little blond girl named Jennifer, built a new home, and diversified their business. Eventually Art gave up farming and entered the business world. Agriculture, of course!

Bev never was too busy for her mother or her father and never outgrew her mothering for her sister Judy. When Judy had her double mastectomy, Bev invited me to lunch (very formally which was unusual) and informed me that she didn't want to hurt my feelings but that she was going to take Judy home with her and take care of her no matter what anyone said. Period!

Bev had had difficulties with her hearing and we were all very worried about it. Her paternal grandfather had been unable to hear a thing without his hearing aid. I was told by his youngest daughter (who had had ear surgery) that the doctor told her that her hearing problem (stapes) was inherited and that the hearing problem was transmitted from son to daughter. In other words, the affliction came from her grandfather through his son (Bev's father) to Bev. Only the girls seemed to have any problem at all! Judy did not inherit this problem, thank the good Lord! Bev told me that she was having problems and we started researching where to go, what to do, and felt that she had reached the right decision when she opted for surgery in St. Louis with a doctor known as the "best in his field."

The surgery was a failure! By the time Bev had adjusted to the fact that she was totally deaf in one ear, it was too late to sue. The doctor really wanted her to sue him I know. It was an error in procedure and he felt so very badly about it. Time passed and Bev managed well with a hearing aid (transmitter) on the good ear with the receiver on the deaf one. You really could not tell that there was anything wrong. We knew it, but no one can really know what it must have been like for her—what it is like for her. She continued to sing in the choir at church (always being sure that the strong voice was on her bad side) and gave good advice about hearing aids to her friends who needed help.

I do not know whether Bev was afraid out on that farm all by herself while Art traveled all over the country in his new job. If she was, she never told us. We worried a great deal about her. Everyone around her knew that she was alone, and, when she slept, she always slept on her good ear and could not hear a thing. I worried more about fire than anything, for she would have never known anything was wrong while she was asleep. Imagine not knowing whether or not someone came into your home—no footsteps, no voice contact, no barking dog—just silence! And not being able to hear a fire alarm or telephones ringing—no sound at all.

Art and Bev moved to North Carolina and she realized one of her lifelong dreams when she bought a boat. She loved boats and had grown up with them at the Lake of the Ozarks. She joined the Coast Guard Auxiliary after a time at the encouragement of her friends and her husband. Art, who still traveled most of the time, knew that she needed something of her own to do while he was away.

Bev wasn't satisfied with that after a while, and with encouragement from the men and women in her flotilla, she decided to try for her pilot's license. This was a big, big step! Much math is needed (not her strongest point), as well as learning tides, maps, and such; all of which I don't understand. She also had the fear that they might not let her take the exam because of her hearing.

Determination? You bet! And, she made it! She got her pilot's license and can even take passengers out into the ocean if she wants to. We are all very proud of her!

Later, she suffered another blow. The hearing in her good ear started to diminish. Again, you can imagine how it must be not to hear normal sounds, water running, footsteps—sounds that we take for granted. Can you even imagine living in a silent world? It is overwhelming for me to even write about it—my beautiful child, this strong woman—and she is handling it with courage. She remains cheerful, never complaining, and I know that she is devastated. I am! Our prayers for her are never-ending.

Once in a great while, Bev and I talk about her problem, but only when she talks about it first. She handles herself so very well that you never feel sorry for her, or feel that she is handicapped. She is an outgoing young woman with a great personality who feels a natural affinity for people. If she cannot hear you, she tells you. She is quite frank about her hearing loss and cheerfully tells you that she doesn't let it be a problem, and it isn't! She has a cute, smart hearing assistant dog and we hope that she never has to depend on him completely. I am happy that she has him, for Art is gone a great deal and she spends so much time alone. Her life has changed in that she has to take her dog, Teaser, everywhere with her. This means restaurants, airplanes, boats—everywhere she goes, Teaser goes with her. Her courage has never faltered and if it has, she never lets you know it! She goes ahead with her usual confidence and courage. If Bev is ever afraid (and I know that at times she has to be) she never lets anyone know it. She goes ahead with that determination to win. She is now the commander of her Coast Guard flotilla and has earned the respect of all of its members! She conducts a strong meeting, follows the Robert's Rules for conducting effective and orderly meetings, makes wise decisions and puts her members and her flotilla first! We are so proud of her! You would enjoy knowing her as she is a delight and an inspiration to us all! She is a winner!

God Bless!

Judith

Judith! The name stands alone and is strong! When my second daughter was born and we named her Judith, my father was so excited and pleased. He told me that it was a Biblical name and that in her story in the Bible, Judith was a heroine, a beautiful, strong woman, and he prayed that my baby daughter would be as strong and as beautiful as her namesake. She is!

Judith Kaye was a darling baby with a ready smile, shy but strong-willed. Stubborn? Perhaps a little, but with her ready, shy smile, who cared? She was born in the month of

January just three days before her father was sworn into the navy. World War II was a reality in our lives. Her big sister, Bee Sue, was fifteen-months old when Judith was born. From the day Judith came home from the hospital until the day her daddy returned from the Pacific she was told about her daddy: how wonderful he was, how he was fighting for his country and for his family and for her. She was told how much he loved her and wanted to see his girls. Bee Sue talked about her daddy to Judy all of the time and they looked forward eagerly to his coming home. Judy was not around men at all, so she was a bit afraid of them, and very shy. When her father did return home after the war, her sister took her by the hand, and they both ran to meet him. There was never a strange moment for Judy, and I did not realize it then, but she has always had the same acceptance of all situations, good and bad.

It is difficult for me to write about the strength and courage of my daughter for I really never knew what she was thinking or feeling. I can only write about how things seemed to be. Jude (that is what we call her most of the time now) has always shown a beautiful sense of humor, a ready smile and a definite opinion about most things. She is not indecisive at all, and it has been good that she is that strong in her beliefs and decisions. As a child, Jude knew how to make herself comfortable in the most uncomfortable surroundings. We always thought that she would be a typical glamour girl who would enjoy all of the comforts of luxury and would not settle for anything less. As I relate some of her story to you, you will see how this ability to adapt and make the most of her surroundings has made life beautiful for her family.

Judy feels things very deeply and cares, really cares about people and about family and loved ones. She never showed much emotion during times of illness and death of loved ones, but would suddenly disappear for a while. Sometimes she became physically ill, and sometimes she would go for a walk and cry alone, grieve alone and do whatever was necessary to face whatever she had to face graciously and with dignity.

During her first year of college, Jude fell in love! We wanted her to finish school before marriage, but she was adamant. She loved Don and wanted to get married. Her courtship was a storybook affair, but I cannot tell you about that. I was not there and it is, after all, her story to tell. Suffice it to say, she was married with all of the pomp and circumstance we could afford at the time, for her father was not well and had not been for some time and we were on a rather tight budget. She made a beautiful bride and a wonderful wife. Whatever Don wanted, she tried to see that he had it, no matter how she had to budget or sacrifice. Did she spoil him? Of course!

I have always said that Jude inherited a great deal of the pioneer spirit of her ancestors. She has an adventuresome spirit and the strength to make things happen. When her husband decided that he wanted to become a teacher, Judith went to work during the day and to school at night in order to become a teacher, also. On a teacher's salary both husband and wife need to work! When he decided that he would like to teach in Australia, their house was rented, household articles sold, visas acquired, reservations made, and Jude, her husband, and their eight-year-old son sailed for Australia. That also makes for another story to tell. It was a beautiful experience for them. They came home after about two-and-a-half-years, and it was so good to have them near me again.

Jude's father had passed away while they were on their way back to the States. She was on a small island where the airplanes only stopped twice a week and was unable to get home for the funeral. This was a very difficult time for her, but she handled the situation very well and if she was having a problem dealing with her grief, no one was aware of it. We did talk about things, she and I, as we usually did and still do when the problems and troubles are big ones—our sensitivity and emotions run deep!

It always seemed to me that when things went along too smoothly and tended to be dull and boring, Jude and Don did something about it. Don had always been an outdoors man and even though he was born a city boy, he had mastered the art of camping, rafting, fishing, and hunting. He dreamed of living in the country where the air is pure, the outdoor sports are available and he could live a quiet, yet productive life. As usual, Jude made it happen! They worked together, planned together and dreamed together. They bought a story-and-a-half log cabin which was over one hundred years old. They took down the cabin log by log (numbering each one) and restored it on a ten acre tract of land that they had purchased in southern Missouri. Jude worked (toiled really) lifting and doing man's work at times so that they could be proud of their cabin in the forest. It could not have been easy, but it was the making of a dream that made it worthwhile. I had had my turn at pioneering and I must have disappointed Jude by my lack of enthusiasm. But I am proud of her courage, strength, determination and most of all, her sense of humor. I don't think I ever told her that!

Her son grew up and was married. Things were going well, and then disaster struck! Judy was told that she had cancer and must have an operation immediately! None of us could believe it! Not our strong, vibrant, healthy Judith! The operation was performed. It was a double mastectomy—a painful, terrible thing to happen to a young woman. It was a physical and an emotional shock to us all! Judy and I talked about it, cried about it and she went back to her small elementary students and told them, "I missed you, and I want you to hug me, but you will have to wait until I don't hurt so much." They understood! As usual, no one knew how much Jude must have suffered and prayed and cried. The only thing she said later to me was, "Remember, Mom, it is the quality of life that is important, not the length of it and I have had a good life." Of course, I cried. I have cried a great deal inside. A mother suffers much more for her children than she does for herself, doesn't she?

Jude is an avid reader with a great desire to keep learning and studying. I doubt if she will ever finish her schooling to her satisfaction. She did get her masters degree plus many extra hours of specialization and psychology. She has used all of that training and education to accomplish many worth-while things. It is very heart-warming to think of the many children and teenagers who will have better lives because of her special teachings and efforts in their behalf. She has done so much work with the emotionally disturbed children and children and young adults with learning disabilities. Plus she has trained the young mentally handicapped how to find employment and make their lives better. It must have been very rewarding work and also very exhausting! It takes a very special person to work with children who are handi-capped in any way, and it requires so much compassion and love! We are all very proud of her!

Time has passed, as it always does, and there have been other mountains to climb. Jude has climbed those mountains with dignity, compassion and love. She has kept her lovely smile and her strength; that special inner strength that makes her such a special person. She is still making things happen when she can and keeps trying when things get difficult. She never gives up! She has two beautiful granddaughters and their relationship is beautiful to see. Judith has shown, to all who know her, great strength and courage. I am so very proud of her and I love her dearly. I pray every day that life will be more easy for her, but whatever comes her way, she will handle it as always—quietly and with great courage!

God Bless!

Mama Bee

I was agonizing over this segment of my writing for it is so difficult to write about oneself. I was afraid that I might exaggerate (which my family tells me I have a tendency to do) and yet, I wanted to present things as they were. My present husband said to me, "Bevie, just do it. You have a lot to tell, and it has made you the person you are today. Just sit down and write it." You decide whether I was strong or whether I became strong through the doing—I will just start the telling!

I suppose that I really started to grow up when Ed, my first husband, went into the service during World War II. I have told this story elsewhere in this book and so will go on to the next growing-up phase of my life. I might mention here, that I feel that we keep growing until we leave this world.

When Ed came home from the navy, he had changed, and so had I. He no longer blindly adored me. Instead he looked at me as I was, with human faults and frailties. Unfortunately, the true image never quite lives up to the dream. He remembered me as I was when he left, and I had changed a great deal.

Our little girls were so happy to have him home, and he thought that they were the most wonderful children in the world. I totally agreed with him. The discipline, the manners, the teaching to tie shoes, dress oneself, and a lot of other simple lessons of life had to come from me. I believe that it usually is this way in most homes. Ed had had a great deal of time to decide what kind of life he wanted to have when he came home. He did not want to work and live in the city. He wanted to live a work-retirement sort of life where he could have a boat. He decided that he wanted to live at the Lake of the Ozarks, so he bought a large service station that could be adapted to include a large collection of fishing supplies, fishing licenses, live bait and a few groceries to sell on Sundays to the tourists checking into their resorts.

I did not want to go! I had made friends with my neighbors and liked it where I lived! It was a rude awakening when I was told, "You and the girls either come with me, or I will go alone!" This from my usually quiet husband was quite a shock! I had been reared to make your husband comfortable, live where he wants to live and so on, so I agreed to move even though I hated the thought of it. Ed was so determined to go that the house was immediately put on the market, and, because it was an inexpensive, small, and fairly-priced home, people started coming by to see it right away. The people who bought our home (and it was a cute house) came by to look at it when I was recovering from an allergic reaction. They stared at my swollen face (I was in bed) and bought it on the spot. Our moving experience makes another story.

We moved into a very tiny house with no bathroom and no hot water, but it did have lots of mice and much togetherness. It was so very small. Suffice it to say, those were the "pioneering days" at the Lake, and we couldn't make enough money to make ends meet. Ed was very frustrated and it must have been very hard for him to give up his dream. One evening at the service station he said, "If it wasn't for you I wouldn't be here working as a gas jockey!" Another shock!

Did I mention that I had learned to operate a gasoline pump, check oil, and the whole bit? I learned very quickly that you do what you have to do in life!

Ed went back to the city to earn a living, and the girls and I stayed at the Lake. The girls were in school and were very happy there. They learned to water ski, went swimming and fishing and loved it all. It was very lonely there that winter. We hadn't realized that everyone went to Florida for the winter. It was much cheaper than winterizing those small, poorly-built houses. There was no doctor nearer than thirty miles, no fire station, no police station; really nothing at all to make a mother of small children feel safe or secure.

And so it was! Ed came home on the weekends. I became involved in the local activities (not everyone could afford Florida), became the president of the Missouri Extension Club and published a cookbook as a fund-raiser. I took on a position as the National Secretary/Treasurer of the Highway

54 Association and did some traveling for them. None of this was really what I wanted to do. I still did the book-work for our business and operated the gasoline pumps, though not as often. We hired a young man to do that work.

The girls and I were quite well-adjusted by this time. They had made many friends at school and were so happy living there. One day I received a telephone call from the school because one of Bev's classmates had told her mother that I had given dancing lessons when I was in high school. It seems that the present dancing teacher had to drive over fifty miles, and he didn't want to continue to do that. Would I consider taking over the class? "Please, please, please, we will do anything you want us to. We want our children to have this advantage," they begged.

I was too stunned to even answer. It had been a few years since I had given lessons, and I had never even considered doing it again. I thought about it and, with great trepidation, agreed. I called my dad who set up a "brush-up" day with a friend of his who taught new routines to the stars. What a grueling weekend that was as I struggled to master months of dancing in one day, but I loved it. It was exciting! I started my new venture with fifteen pupils and promised them a recital if they really worked and practiced. They did and I did! We had over three hundred people attend the recital, and, before I knew it, I had over three hundred students. The schools in the Lake area gave me keys to their gyms because they wanted the children in the area to have their chance to learn. The school my girls attended let me use their school for the recitals.

So it began and we all loved it! It was the most rewarding experience I have ever had! The only drawback to all of this was that now I had one more job. I did the book-work, manned the cash register at the service station and the sporting goods area when necessary, and I did the necessary tax work. Taking care of my girls was not work to me. I loved them and it was my pleasure.

I have one regret about those few years and that is that I didn't have as much time to spend with them as I would have liked. When Ed came home for weekends with guests, I was really too tired to enjoy him or them. When I began to resent the extra work they caused, I decided it was time for us to go back to the city. I hated to do that; we all were so happy there! But I wanted my children to have some of the advantages of city life, and I felt that it was crucial to my marriage for me to do so. I canceled the dancing lessons with the promise to come back for the recital we had planned, and we moved back to St. Louis. It was another difficult adjustment! We were never as carefree and happy as we had been in the Ozarks, and the girls missed their freedom and their many friends. I realized that in our years of marriage, Ed and I had not really lived a normal married life. We had not spent much time together at all. He was not used to the day by day responsibility of a family, and I was not used to sharing decisions! It was hard for all of us!

While we were living at the Lake, my only brother who was so special to all of us and who had a special God-given musical ability, passed away suddenly. He was thirty-six-years old. We were all devastated! Mother and Dad took his older boy who was about eight years old and my sister-in-law's brother adopted his youngest boy. His mother did not want them but that, too, is another story. It was hard for my parents to cope with a child again so, when Tony became ill, Mother called me. He had polio and because he had more than one kind, it was almost impossible to diagnose. After spending a week in isolation with him, we took him to Chicago for special care. He lived, thank God, and I came home to my family again.

Ed had been wonderful, taking care of his girls and managing everything. When I came home, I went to work as a cashier in the service department at Weber Chevrolet, and, from there, I was put in charge of their insurance department. This was to be a part-time position, but I was there every day.

Bev and Judy were in school at City House, a private Catholic school. We were not of the Catholic faith, but we were recommended by a very good friend. The school agreed to accept our girls after Bev and Jude took scholastic tests. We were all living in an artist's studio home at that time which was very interesting, but I did not feel really settled until we bought a home. We were limited because Ed did not want to have to drive too far to work and so we sort of agreed to compromise. It was a nice, big, old, three-story home in a settled neighborhood—a home that lent itself to gracious living and was nice to entertain in. We enjoyed it, although I never could accept that it was really my home forever. I quit my job at Weber and looked forward to enjoying being a wife and mother!

Then another shock!

Dad called one Sunday when we had just come home from church. "Can you come? Your mother has had a stroke and she needs you; I need you!" I drove to Farina that very day leaving Ed in charge. I nursed mother for about three weeks. I had never realized how helpless my dad was under trying circumstances, and it was very difficult. Mother's disposition had changed so much, and she was so resentful of me because I had her on the diet that the doctor recommended. My own doctor told me later that strokes often changed a person's disposition. I wish I had known that at the time.

Mother recovered almost completely except for the disposition change. I came home and our life resumed for a short time. Then Ed came home one day with what we assumed was a touch of the flu. He got worse, however, so we took him to the hospital. His exploratory operations, his terribly long stay at the hospital—everything!—were extremely stressful. During that time, I discovered that my deep faith in God was real! I had always wondered. I had grown up a Christian, but I had no idea how strong my faith really would be in an emergency.

One night I prayed, "Please help me, oh Lord, make my husband live, and if it be Thy will to take him, please give me the strength to bear it." I knew I was a true believer. God answered my prayers, and Ed recovered, though he would never again be the strong, virile young man that he had been. Ed was put to bed for six months of bed rest, and I became very active in the Daughters of the American Revolution in order to have something other than nursing as an interest. While he needed constant nursing we realized that I couldn't cope with the steps in that big house so we moved into a smaller home in Ladue. He still wouldn't move very far from the office so it was another "make do" home. I liked it but didn't have a feeling of permanency there either.

Time passed, and we did a little entertaining. The family came at Christmas; our last Christmas together. My dad wasn't feeling well due to arthritis in his back, and my folks decided to go home early. My dad had cancer. My mother couldn't cope and I went back again to Farina to care for Dad. I drove over every Monday and came home again on Friday for the weekend to be with my family. It was so hard physically, but much harder emotionally, to know that I was needed in two places. It was also very hard to watch my beloved father suffer so with no chance of recovery.

Ed's doctor told me that I was needed at home, and we managed the best we could although I know Bev and Judy must have felt very neglected. They were wonderful about it all, and I have always felt that they learned to cope at an early age, because they had the strength to do so. They went to Farina with me during the school vacation. My caring, sensitive, darling dad passed away, and, as soon as I could leave my mother, I came back home to care for my family. If all of these crises sound too depressing, I must tell you that we had our very happy times, too. I am only relating the stories that I feel helped me develop strength and courage.

The girls married and Ed and I settled into a routine way of living. He had a slight stroke from which he recovered completely, and then he had a massive coronary. He knew that he was having a heart attack even though he had no pain. It was frightening and difficult. He felt that God had deserted him. He recovered as much as one can from a massive heart attack and it was bed rest time again! I think that I dislike television today because I had to watch so much of it with Ed. "Shoot-em-ups" were the order of the day.

The grandchildren were born, beautiful children, and we both adored them. Judy had a son, Tim, and Bev had a daughter, Jennifer. They were and are wonderful! We had good years visiting Judy and family in Australia and spending weekends on the farm with Bev and her family. Ed was feeling much better and felt that we had some good years ahead of us together.

Mother had another stroke and this time had to go to the hospital. I spent much time driving back and forth to the hospital in Vandalia, Illinois to spend a little time with her. I had her moved to my sister's home near Chicago in order that my sister could care for her for a while, but she didn't live long. She was lost without her husband, Glenn.

Not long after my mother's death, my brother-in-law called me with the news that my sister had cancer and didn't have long to live. Edythe, my sister, was my staunch supporter. No matter what I did, she thought I was the greatest. When I was elected to the State Board of the DAR, she wrote a beautiful letter telling me how proud she was and how much she admired me. I was sick at the thought of her suffering, and I didn't think I could bear the thought of losing her. I traveled to Tinley Park, Illinois every week to see her and, toward the end, spent several days with her before she returned to the hospital. She did not sleep so we talked all night, remembering our childhood, our wonderful family times when our family was living. I am glad I was with her when she died.

I felt so all alone. I couldn't believe I felt that way when I had such a beautiful, caring family. I realized that there was no one left who thought I was wonderful no matter what I did or did not do! I was now the "older generation."

Ed and I often discussed his fragile health, but he was feeling so much better that he said to me, "I think if I am careful, I will probably live another ten years." We went to Festus, Missouri to visit friends for the weekend, and, in the middle of the night, Ed had another massive heart attack! We both felt differently about this one. I can't say why, but when I visited him in intensive care, he said, "I guess you are really praying, aren't you?"

All I could say was "Yes, I am." And then he was gone!

The three years of widowhood were difficult ones because I was the first in my group of friends to face the death of a mate. We were comparatively young, and no one really knew how to help me. I was invited to the large parties, but day-by-day living completely alone was a problem that I had to cope with by myself. I never dreamed that I would pose a threat to my married friends, or that I would lose friends because of my single status! It was another learning experience! I learned that you have to deal with everything by yourself and that no matter how busy you keep yourself during the day, when you came home at night, you are completely alone. No one really wanted to hear about my troubles, and I couldn't blame them. I felt that I had adjusted very well, but my daughters would not agree with that statement.

Just when I had decided that I would spend the rest of my life alone and that I would have to adjust to that, I met Roy! My love! This is another story—a love story—and I don't know the ending to this one! Our years together have been very special; I am blessed!

God Bless!

The Wonderful Story of Natalie

The ways of the Lord are strange indeed, and, if we have faith and confidence, His ways work wonders for us. I want to tell you the story of Natalie, one of God's miracles! A true blessing for the whole family!

Randy and Sherrie wanted a baby of their own so badly. The child would complete their togetherness as a family. Randy is Roy's son, and Sherrie is our daughter-in-law. Their love for one another was so great, you had to see them together to understand their feelings for one another. They were so happy; they really didn't need anyone else in their lives, but they felt that they were so blessed that they wanted to share their happiness with a child of their own to continue their heritage of love and sharing.

Prayers, doctors, and medication notwithstanding, no one could help them, and they had to accept the fact that they could not have children. They decided to adopt a baby! This had to be a very great decision for them to make! We were delighted! This proved to be a very long and involved process and they left no stone unturned before they decided to put their plans for adoption on hold. They wanted this child while they were still young enough to enjoy it but knew that this was a lengthy process.

One day, while I was having lunch with a dear friend (we shared many confidences), Mary asked me how the adoption process was going for Randy and Sherrie. I told her that while they had not lost hope, they were going to wait for a while because it was so disappointing and so emotionally difficult for them. We chatted for a while when Mary suddenly said, "Bevie, have the children considered adopting a child from another country?" I must have stared at her for a while. I had not thought of that at all and I did not know whether or not they had! Mary then went on to tell me about the young lady in her church in Bourbon, Missouri who had adopted three little girls from Russia. She said that they were beautiful and asked me if I would like to have a picture of them. Of course, I answered yes. I went home quite excited about the idea of adoption from another country, yet a little apprehensive about it, too. I did not mention the idea to anyone.

The picture came with these beautiful little blonde girls. I was surprised to see the blond hair. I had thought all Russians were dark-haired. I called Randy and Sherrie immediately. Sherrie was out of town, and Randy said that he would mention the idea of an adoption from Russia to her. I was not trying to force this idea upon them, so I told him that if they were interested, just let me know and I would send them the picture. Randy called me later and told me that Sherrie was not too enthused with the idea right now, so I stuck the picture into my desk drawer and forgot about it.

A month or so later, I found the picture while cleaning out my desk and I called Randy. "Randy," I said, "I still have the picture of the little Russian girls. Should I throw it away, or shall I send it on to you? They are pretty children and you might like to see this picture of them."

"Yes," Randy answered, "I would like to take a look at the picture." And so, I mailed it to him. I didn't hear from them for a while and then one day I received a telephone call from Sherrie.

"Bevie, I am so excited! We are going to adopt a little girl from Russia. For the first time in years, I am not crying myself to sleep, and we owe it all to you." Then she told me about the procedures, all time consuming and very costly, and then said, "I don't care if it takes all of the money we have saved, it will be worth it! I am so excited, we both are!" And so it was!

Time passed and finally the day arrived when we took Randy and Sherrie to the airport to catch the plane for Russia where they would pick up Natalie. We had already seen her pictures. Their adventures in Russia make another interesting story. We were on hand at the airport to pick up this beautiful, blessed new family when they returned. There were other families there for the same reason.

This child is very special! She held her arms out to us and was immediately "at home" with her new relatives. Sherrie told me that when they arrived at the orphanage and were put into the little room to wait for their new daughter, she was very nervous and didn't quite know how to handle meeting her daughter for the very first time. The door opened, and in walked Natalie (two years old). When Sherrie held out her hands, Natalie walked right into her arms and held on. This was her new world, and understanding what was happening or not, she was not going to let go! God surely does work in mysterious ways, does He not? We are all so very blessed. What a wonderful new world for Natalie! She is a treasure!

God Bless!

I Am Growing Older

The other day I realized that there were some changes that must be made, and soon, for I am growing older. The time will come before I realize it when I am no longer productive. When I reach that stage, I must be prepared to handle reality gracefully. This will be very difficult for me; I have never faced reality "straight on" but have handled events—good or bad—as seems best at the time. I have listed some of my proposed changes and list them just in case the shoe fits. You might want to re-evaluate yourself, as I am trying to do by this writing.

1. I must stop talking too much! I really do not have to expound on every topic that arises, do I?
2. I must not criticize! The world is a different one than I grew up in! It is time for me to realize that!
3. I must stop suggesting opposite viewpoints to keep the conversation alive. By all means, I must watch what I say for things do not always come out the way I expect them to!
4. I must straighten my closets for the comfort and efficiency of others.

5. I must not expect others to like me or all of the things that I do. I must quit grousing and spending time feeling sorry for myself because I am old. I am alive! God loves me! What more do I have to have?!

When I have reached the non-productive time of life, I must relax and enjoy! I have had a beautiful life, even with all of its troubles, sorrows and pain. Now is the time to let go and let the world around me get on with things. Others will decide what to do. It's their turn, let them! Is having my way that important in my life? No, it is not. I must do the things that I feel are necessary, and then play a bit, read a lot, shop, or sleep and perhaps dream. Daydreaming is a very pleasant past time. I must remember that the world can go on without any of us. I must not feel sorry for myself because I am growing older. I have had my time in the sun and now I must count my blessings. I truly am blessed with beautiful children and I love them! I also have beautiful step-children and I love them, too! A special bonus of beautiful grandbabies and great-grandbabies, plus, a wonderful, wonderful husband, lover, friend, and companion! In the vernacular of today, I must "get real!" I have had and still have a good life. It is better than most! I feel that with God's help, I have earned it. Has it cost me too much? Not at all! I am still so young to me and have so much more yet to do. I don't really believe I will ever grow old!

God Bless!

Remember the Good Times

I couldn't completely finish my moment with you until I had told you of the good times and added a few of my special prayers. We all have a tendency to speak of the difficult years or the tragedies; I am guilty of this. I have always regretted the fact that all of the members of my family spent the last few years of their lives being terribly unhappy. Perhaps I have been wrong in my thinking and God was removing them from all of this—taking them home. May I now share some of the happy times and how I now remember my loved ones?

In my very young years, I can remember so well the love and support of my mother and my daddy, and we had fun together. Mother would help me with my recitations, and I had many of them. In a small village if you show any talent at all, you are called upon to perform quite often. I think my talent was having the confidence (or sheer nerve) to face a crowd of people and show off. At any rate, mother encouraged me and was never too busy to work with me. She taught me to emphasize and develop expression in speaking, in my gestures and in my facial expressions. I loved it all! Dad taught me how to "clog," and I was doing soft-shoe routines before I even knew what to call them or that I was really dancing. My brother taught me how to keep in time to the music; my sister was my very special audience. I realize now what a lucky little girl I was. They were happy times!

Our home was a warm welcoming oasis for all of our friends; they were welcome at any time of the day or night if they needed someone to share their happiness or their problems with. I can vividly remember one late evening (about 2:00 A.M.) when a group of Dad's friends stopped by on their way home from a hunting trip. Mother and Dad, as usual, were the gracious host and hostess, and mother prepared some of the game. The hunters' wives were called, and a memory was created as a spur-of-the-moment late-night dinner party occurred. There were always people at our home; everyone loved to be there where they received a warm welcome and were greeted with warm laughter and affection.

I remember so well the evenings that Mother and Dad took us to the formal dances at nearby towns. Dad could play almost any musical instrument by ear though he could not read a note. As a hobby and an outlet for his love of music, he organized evenings of dancing and brought well-known orchestras into these communities. It was an exciting time and many of the people we met in the music world became quite famous. My sister and I never had to learn how to dance for we had always known how. Dad used to tell us that if we just followed the lead of our partner, we could never fail to be one of the best.

On cold winter evenings we sat in our living room, each with our own favorite book or sometimes extra schoolwork, and we spent the time together. Many times our parents told us stories of their childhood, their romantic elopement and their fun trips with friends. Often we shared those trips with their friends and families; it was a small community with much caring and sharing and concern for everyone. They were happy years! We were encouraged and helped in every way and if there wasn't always money to "make things happen" we were encouraged to keep trying and find a way, which we usually did.

In other chapters in my book, I have told of other happenings, but I want to encourage you all, by the telling to remember the good times in your life. The road of life can be very difficult, almost impossible, and at times you don't think you can "make it" or "face it." But, there is always an answer! God is with you! There is always prayer! His answer may be found in the helping hand of a friend, a telephone call, a letter in the mail, the love of your family; remember that it is always there! Remember that whatever you do, it affects someone else. When you laugh and are happy, everyone who loves you is also happy; when you cry those who love you are unhappy, too. The "sticky patches" in life are a part of living and you can get through them by working at it, but you must also keep a positive and happy attitude. Remember the happy times; everyone has some of those. Remember those times with a smile, a tear, a laugh, but always with gratitude and love for having them in your life.

God bless!

Special Prayers

I cannot remember a time when I did not pray, but my prayers were a very personal and private part of my life. I did not realize until I was a grown woman that people need prayers—prayers said aloud just for their problems and needs. It wasn't until I was asked to be the Chaplain of the Missouri State Society, Daughters of the American Revolution, and duly elected, that I began to use special words to try to touch the hearts of those who were gathered together at our meetings. The more I studied about the men and women who gave their lives and fortunes to establish "one nation, under God," the more I understood and realized that God is there for us every minute of every day. Believing that, you can face anything that happens to you.

I was so blessed to have that office. I gained so much and strengthened my faith so greatly that I was able and am able to face life's adversities and cope even though I might want to sit down and quit. God is there for me, and I know that I can do what I have to do. Everyone carries a burden, but it is invisible, and no one may know that you are carrying it. Prayers are always welcome and always needed.

I became the Christian Growth Chairman of my church, and my devotion to my prayers was strengthened. I have

been asked so many times by my friends to put my prayers into a book and so here are some of them, just for you. I will say to you as I have always said in the past, "Will you pray with me?"

A New Day

Lord, thank you for giving me this beautiful new day. May I never take for granted this precious life that you have given to me. Teach me to enjoy every moment of it and to share some of that joy with others I might meet along the way. The burdens that I carried yesterday, Lord, are much lighter this morning; some of them have even disappeared. I am grateful to you. I pray that I may never take my many blessings for granted, Lord, and that I will always share them with others. Keep me safe this day, I pray, and before this day ends may I make someone else a little happier and their way a little easier. These things I pray in Thy name, Amen.

Facing Challenges

Lord, I am so grateful for the opportunity to meet this new challenge and to travel into the future down life's road. May I accept this challenge and be a good example to others as I strive to succeed and attain this goal. May I reach out to help others along the way; to do some act of kindness; to always remember that no one works alone for you are with me. Help me, dear Lord, to face the dark and dreary days with a cheerful smile and to be grateful for the bright and beautiful days. Help me use this day of opportunity, filled with determination to use this, my life, to help and improve myself and my fellow men. Amen.

Help Me Grow

Dear Lord, I need your help that I may broaden my vision so that I might see all things and grow in knowledge.

I know that of all possessions, knowledge is the best, for no one can steal it. It has more value than anyone can estimate, and it cannot be destroyed by anyone. Grant me, Lord, wisdom, tolerance and understanding; help me have a cheerful smile, a helping hand, and to know right from wrong as I strive to be strong and true in everything I say and do every day. These things I pray, Amen.

My Prayer For Today

Oh Lord, what have you planned for me today? Show me where love and hope and faith are needed, and use me to bring them to those places. Grant me, I pray, strength through my adversities and compassion for those who need it. Help me to remember that love ever gives and forgives. I know, Lord, that there will never be another now, so help me make the most of today. Guide me as I face tomorrow for I know not what the future will hold, and I would hope that I can weave some beautiful memories for my friends and loved ones. May I have a smile, a kind word, or a special thought for each and every one I meet today. These things I pray in Thy name, Amen.

My Prayer For Me

Lord, help me to remember that nothing is going to happen to me today that you and I together cannot handle. Help me think clearly; help me plan my work so that I may have time to play, to read, to laugh, to dream and to worship. Remind me, Lord, that I must not be too busy to be kind and loving to my family, and, as my day goes forward, remind me, also to pray for those who need your help or who are lonely and afraid. Remind me that I must show my appreciation for the love and friendship given to me for no one knows how much it means unless I tell them so! Thank you, Lord, for this day you have given to me. Help me to do

Thy will with a happy heart and hands that are willing. These things I pray in Thy name, Amen.

A Prayer of Thanksgiving

Dear Lord, we thank Thee for the tears and the smiles of life, the small and the weak, the big and the strong. Help us remember the dear friends who are no longer with us, who have blessed us with their friendship. Help us to remember them with fondness and love. We thank Thee for our blessings and our testing times, too. We thank Thee for the beauty of the trees and flowers, a child's happy smile, a loving hug and a friendly "hello." We need Thee, Lord; we need to believe and to know that only love can turn the rain to rainbows everywhere. We thank Thee for that. We give thanks for the love of family and friends. Help us to look ahead with joy and laughter and to keep dreaming and to live every day all of the days of our lives. All of these things we pray in Thy name, Amen.